Parenting a Grieving Child

REVISED EDITION

Parenting a Grieving Child

HELPING CHILDREN FIND FAITH, HOPE,
AND HEALING AFTER THE LOSS OF
A LOVED ONE

Mary DeTurris Poust

LOYOLA PRESS.
A JESUIT MINISTRY
Chicago

LOYOLA PRESS.
A JESUIT MINISTRY

3441 N. Ashland Avenue
Chicago, Illinois 60657
(800) 621-1008
www.loyolapress.com

Scripture quotations are from New Revised Standard Version Bible: Catholic Edition, copyright © 1989, 1993 National Council of the Churches of Christ in the United States of America. Used by permission. All rights reserved.

Cover art credit: Eri Morita/Media Bakery.

ISBN-13: 978-0-8294-4256-4
ISBN-10: 0-8294-4256-1
Library of Congress Control Number: 2015939791

Printed in the United States of America.

15 16 17 18 19 20 Versa 10 9 8 7 6 5 4 3 2 1

To my mother, Irene DeTurris,
whose absence I will mourn and
whose life I will celebrate
all of my days.

And to my husband, Dennis,
and our children, Noah, Olivia, and Chiara,
whose love and enthusiasm
fill me with joy
and make my life complete.

Contents

Introduction

We live in a culture where people are willing to talk about a lot of personal things, probably more than we should, but there's one topic that still remains taboo: death. When the first edition of this book came out in 2002, people I knew—parents of young children, friends with aging parents, people who knew all too well the reality of grief in their own lives—would tell me time and again, "I don't need that book." And I think they really believed it, or wanted to believe it, because none of us wants to face the fact that we will all need this book, or one very much like it, eventually.

When it comes to grief, we are all experts or on our way to being so. The time to think about death and what we believe about it is before we ever need a book like this, long before, but that's no easy sell. It seems macabre to think about death before it makes itself known in the landscape of our lives. Why dwell on darkness before its time has come? However, if we wait until a moment of crisis, it's often too difficult to sort out our true feelings and beliefs in the midst of grief.

For parents stuck in that moment and trying to help their children wrestle with grief at the same time, it's critical to have "helpers" who can put the resources they need directly into their hands. They need spiritual support and practical tools, but in a time of crisis they often don't have the strength or the ability to find that help for themselves.

Whether you are a helper or a parent trying to guide a child through grief, I'm hoping this book will be the first step on that long road. I know from experience that it's not easy to face the loss of someone we love, or explain it to a child. Death can leave us paralyzed. We wake up and wonder how we will get out of bed, face another day, or take another breath. To know that we can't protect the children we love from those same sorrows and struggles is almost too much to bear, and so we convince ourselves that we don't need to think about it or talk about it. Until we do.

Every child—just like every adult—grieves on his or her own terms. Personalities, family dynamics, relationships, and spirituality: these factors that make each one of us an individual also allow each one of us to grieve in a unique way. There are no hard-and-fast parameters for what grief will look like and how long it will last. If there is any universal truth regarding children and grief, it is that the adults who love and care for these children must be prepared for and open to a wide range of reactions. We may not understand or approve, but we can try to find ways to be nonjudgmental and supportive so that our children will feel comfortable grieving on their own terms.

In the pages of this book, real parents who have faced real sorrows share their stories and offer practical and thoughtful ways to help children cope with death. You also will find advice from doctors, therapists, funeral directors, chaplains, teachers, counselors, and others who have witnessed the powerful process death sets in motion for those left behind. In addition, there are activities at the end of each chapter—reflection questions, meditations, and more—to help adults and children alike come to terms with loss, death, grief, and healing.

You can begin this book at chapter 1 and read it all the way through, or you can open it to whichever chapter most suits your needs and begin reading there. I hope it will serve as a manual, a reference book, a spiritual guide, and an emotional comfort to all those struggling to help children understand death.

Whether you are a parent, a relative, a friend, a teacher, a babysitter, or another adult who knows a child facing the journey through grief, the time to start talking about it is now. Grief doesn't go away. It may hide, but it remains present, and a child who isn't given the opportunity to walk that path openly and with support will suffer for it one way or another.

We take away some of death's power to paralyze when we talk about it honestly. It should never be a taboo subject, even where children are concerned. Death, as our faith teaches us, is another part of life, a doorway to eternity, and we will all walk that path one day.

1

Children Will Grieve
—With or Without You

- The power of our first death memories
- Your memories, their healing
- What every parent fears
- Every loss matters
- How deep is the hurt?
- Where does faith fit in?
- Grief and mourning—is there a difference?
- Talking about death

> *Nothing can make up for the absence of someone we love. . . . We must simply hold out and see it through.*
> —Dietrich Bonhoeffer, *Letters and Papers from Prison*

I was only five years old when my grandfather died of a heart attack in a local bowling alley. I remember that October day like it was yesterday. I can see myself sitting in the backseat of my grandmother's big white car as she drove up to the front of her house, only to find a priest and the next-door neighbors waiting outside on the porch. It's a wonderfully vivid memory. Unfortunately, none of it is true. It is the creation of a child's imagination, an imagination that was left to make its own memories when there wasn't enough reality to explain the confusion and sadness all around.

My grandfather's death was a mystery to me. One day he was there—pushing me in my swing in the willow tree in his backyard, teasing me relentlessly as we ate lunch together, convincing me that the booming thunder that sent me running to his big brown armchair was God bowling in the attic. The next day he was gone. No one gave me any details. No one told me what was happening. All I knew was that now when I knelt down to say my prayers before bed, I asked God to bless "Grandpa in heaven" instead of plain old Grandpa.

But heaven can be a pretty hard concept to grasp, especially when you're five years old and the only loss you've experienced is watching your best friend move away. I didn't know where heaven was or what it meant that my grandfather was going there. Because I wasn't allowed to attend his wake or funeral, I never really understood that he was gone for good. For a couple of years after his death, I expected him to show up in church on Sunday. I knew my family had gone there to say good-bye, so it seemed only logical that he would return there eventually.

It wasn't until I was older that I realized that the big, gray stone at the cemetery, the one engraved with praying hands and my last name, was Grandpa's grave. I was seven when it finally dawned on me that Grandpa wasn't coming back on Sunday morning or any other day.

When my mother died of cancer twenty years later, my aunt asked me if she should allow my five-year-old cousin to attend the wake and funeral. I told her about my experience and encouraged her to let him go if that was what he wanted. The result was truly an eye-opener for me. Not only did Gregory want to go to the wake, but he ended up being a comfort to the adults around him.

I remember how he bravely walked up to the casket with my Aunt Margaret at his side. He looked at my mother and told my tearful aunt, "Don't cry, Mommy. Aunt Irene is happy now." It was all the proof needed to convince me that children cannot be separated from the grieving process. They are aware of the sadness and mourning around them when someone dies, and they need to understand the reason for that sadness if they are ever going to move beyond it and begin to heal. But that's no small feat, especially for a small child.

The power of our first death memories

The human mind is powerful and clever. It can protect us from memories that are too painful to remember by blocking them completely from our interior view. It can provide new, although sometimes inaccurate, memories to fill in the gaps that leave us unsettled or confused. It can strengthen or intensify memories of good things so that those memories anchor us when we feel adrift. Too often though, if we aren't given the time, space, and support we need to grieve after the death of a loved one, the mind can hold us down and keep us in a place of sadness, doubt, fear, and pain. Children—from infants to young adults—are no different from adults on that count, except for the fact that they can't traverse the rocky terrain of grief on their own.

They need the help of the adults around them, and that's where you come in.

If you are a teacher or principal, guidance counselor or school secretary, chaplain or pastoral minister, day care worker or babysitter—if you work regularly with children in any capacity at all—you play a critical role in their healthy grieving. Everything you do to help on this front complements what parents might be doing at home. And sometimes, when a parent is too distraught to do anything at all, you may be the only lifeline a child can grab onto when he is treading, all alone, the murky waters of mourning.

Before any of us can guide a child successfully through grief, however, we have to reflect on, and come to terms with, our own death-related memories, religious beliefs, and spiritual questions. Each one of us brings our own story to the table, even if we don't realize it. Somewhere, perhaps lurking in the depths of our subconscious, is an experience or a conversation or book or movie that colored our feelings about death, for better or, more often, for worse. By digging deep into those thoughts and feelings we bring to the surface everything we need as a starting point for helping a child in grief: our own hard-won narrative on this difficult subject.

Your memories, their healing

Try to remember the first time you were exposed to death. Was it a friend, a relative, someone who was part of your daily life, or a distant uncle you hardly knew? Maybe it wasn't a real death experience at all. Perhaps you watched a movie or read a book where a beloved character died. Or maybe you saw a news report of some tragic death that made you realize for the first time that children die, or parents die, or people are killed by illnesses or bullets or storms.

The children in your care build their views of death in the very same way. What makes it especially challenging for you as a helper is the fact that every child has a different story, a different foundation of faith, and a different family attitude toward death and dying. There is no one-size-fits-all approach to grief and mourning.

I didn't learn that my vivid recollections of my grandfather's death were false until I started doing the research for this book. All those years I thought I had been there, a witness to my grandmother's initial shock and grief, but I had never really verified it. Back then, talking about death or about dead people was a taboo subject on the Italian side of my family. So I took snippets of what people said and crafted my own story—a common practice among children who do not get all the information they need.

When I made my first communion in second grade, I was given a small pendant with a pair of praying hands on it, hands that matched the ones on my grandfather's tombstone. For me, that necklace became a kind of link. It reminded me of him, and that was all I needed to turn it into a keepsake of the time we had spent together. Even now I keep a worn, pig-shaped cutting board on display in my kitchen because it reminds me of the lunches I shared with my grandfather. These little physical remembrances may not seem like much, but they are telltale signs of how powerfully loss affects us. We want those around us to recognize our grief, and we want a way to keep the memory of our loved one alive.

What kind of memories does your first death experience stir up? If you reflect on that question, your answer will serve as a guidepost when you need to lead the children in your classroom, hospital, Scout troop, parish, or home down the road to healing.

What every parent fears

No parent wants to have to talk to their young child about death. It seems scary at best, cruel at worst. Parents are hardwired to want to protect their children from anything that will upset them or lead to those middle-of-the-night, scared-of-the-dark fears and nightmares. And so, many parents put off the inevitable, convincing themselves that saying nothing until necessary is the best approach. That puts children in the vulnerable position of being surprised by death, because one way or another, death will occur, if not in their own tight-knit world then in their peripheral one.

For some children the loss of a sibling will turn life upside down. For others it may be the death of an aged grandparent, an ill parent, a beloved friend, or a faithful pet. Children are deeply affected by the death of a loved one, regardless of who it is or how it happens. Although different kinds of deaths may cause different kinds of reactions, no loss is ever easy. Any loss can be a major loss to a child. Depending on a child's age, grief reactions can range from mild sadness to physical illness to powerful shifts toward aggressive behavior or to complete withdrawal. Grief reactions will also be influenced by the kind of relationship a child had with the deceased, and her understanding of death before the loss occurred.

Although I never said a word to my parents, as a child I secretly wondered about my grandfather's disappearance from my life. I overheard stories that scared me and fed my imagination. There were tales of relatives fainting at the wake, of smelling salts, of endless crying. There was the long mourning period, which I don't remember but which surely had an impact on me. How many afternoons can a five-year-old sit at her grandmother's house with no radio, no television, and no laughter? My sister, who was only six months old when our grandfather died, cried every time someone sang "Happy Birthday" well into her childhood. As best we can guess, that response stemmed from her seeing our family members crying at every birthday and holiday celebration in the years after Grandpa died.

My first experience with death influenced all my subsequent experiences with death and the way I now handle the subject with my own children. Ever since my children were very young, I have talked to them openly and honestly about death whenever the subject comes up. If we're paying attention, it will come up more often than we might expect. Between the fictional deaths found in books and movies and the all-too-real deaths seen on the news and social media, children are exposed again and again to things that can trigger questions. These "teachable moments" are perfect opportunities to talk about death, or at least about life. And despite how it may appear on the surface, that's not a bad thing.

My nine-year-old daughter, Chiara, sat at the kitchen table one morning with tears in her eyes. She told us that she had been lying awake in bed at night and thinking about a story she'd seen on the news weeks before, when my husband and I were overseas and she was at home with her grandparents. When we asked what the story was about, she told us, with some hesitation, that it was about "a son who killed his father." His mother didn't know why the boy did it, she added, looking at us as if we could undo what she had heard, reverse this awful thing with the same parent-type magic that heals toddler boo-boos with a kiss and soothes childhood nightmares with a glass of water and a light left on in the hallway.

I wanted to cry, too, as I imagined Chiara wide awake and fearful while we were unaware. I held her on my lap and smoothed her hair. My husband, Dennis, explained that sometimes people have mental illnesses that make them do very bad things but that this young man couldn't hurt her or us. She wasn't afraid of being hurt by him; she was scared by the prospect that things like this could ever happen. Anywhere. This story had taken on a life of its own in her mind, in part because we were far away and she was probably already fearful that something might happen to us. That's how death gets under our skin and into our heads. It takes one scary thing and puts another on top of it until it paralyzes us or keeps us up at night. The way to defuse that ticking time bomb is to talk honestly, to bring in faith, to reassure and move the fear from center stage, where it is taking on too much power, to its rightful place alongside all the happy stories and good memories. That doesn't mean we hide the truth or gloss over terrible things. Quite the opposite. We uncover and reveal, answering questions and calming fears as they arise. We create an environment—at home, in the classroom, in day care—where children feel comfortable asking questions about the things that make them afraid.

Every loss matters

We may assume that there is some sort of hierarchy of grieving scenarios. Is it worse to lose a parent than a grandparent? Is it more painful to lose a sibling to a car accident than to leukemia? The reality is that whatever loss a child is grieving right now is the worst possible loss that child can fathom. It does not matter that it was the expected death of a girl's ninety-five-year-old grandma. It is still the death of a beloved friend who used to tell her stories in the afternoon.

Donna Schuurman, chief executive officer of the Dougy Center, a grief support program in Portland, Oregon, says that comparisons don't come into play when a child is grieving. What matters is the relationship the child had with the deceased person. "If that grandparent was really instrumental in her life, she's not going to think, 'Old people die. It's better than losing my sixteen-year-old friend.' She's going to think, 'I've lost someone in my life who is not going to be there anymore—and that hurts.' It doesn't become a comparative process. The worst loss is the one you are experiencing."

That same philosophy applies when it comes to the way a loved one dies. A judgment of better or worse just doesn't matter when we're talking about life and death. Is sudden death by car accident, for example, somehow worse for a child to deal with than the loss of a loved one due to an extended illness? Yes, there can be an incompleteness when someone dies suddenly. There are no opportunities to say good-bye, to end an argument, to say what needs to be said. On the other hand, although long-term illness provides an opportunity to prepare for the death, it can also bring other hardships for the survivors. People often don't look like themselves after an extended illness. They may even lose their mental capabilities, making it especially difficult for children to cope.

"It doesn't really matter how the loved one died," says Schuurman. "Imagine saying to a kid, 'At least your father died of cancer and not in a car accident.' What point does that make? You can actually have a kid whose father dies of suicide and a kid whose father dies in a car accident, and the one who's dealing with the suicide is doing much better."

How deep is the hurt?

So how do we know how badly children are hurting? For one thing, we need to be open to the possibility that they may be grieving deeply over a loss we consider fairly insignificant. We are all affected by death in very different ways. When was the last time you looked at the obituary page and stopped to read about the life and death of someone you never even met? Death moves us. Death scares us. Death makes us think about all the what-ifs.

Children may not approach death in such a conscious way, but they do take in the seriousness of what is happening around them, even though they often do so in thoroughly self-centered ways. A child who loses a parent will typically run through a laundry list of questions such as: *How will this affect me? What happens now? Am I going to be able to go to college? Who's going to teach me how to drive? Will I ever be able to go camping again?* It isn't until later that the child will start to notice more significant things, like the fact that her father, who died at age forty-two, won't ever get to experience the rest of his life, that he lost out on the chance to raise his children, grow old with his wife, achieve his career goals, and meet his grandchildren. So we have to meet children where they are, even if where they are seems remarkably self-absorbed and not at all what we expect of someone who is grieving.

While every loss affects a child in a meaningful way, there is no doubt that certain losses affect a child in devastating ways. We can talk about the uniqueness of every child. We can even talk about how one child may handle the loss of a parent better than another handles the loss of a friend. But the bottom line is that some deaths have the power to incapacitate children.

For children who live at home with their parents and siblings, the loss of a mother, father, brother, or sister is about as devastating as it gets. Having lost my own mother when I was twenty-five years old, I can assure anyone who has never lost a parent that this was about as painful an experience as I could ever imagine at that point in my life.

She was my mother, after all, but she was also much more than that. She was my confidante, my best friend, and my hero. I could not imagine my life without her. There were many times not long after her death when I picked up the phone to call her with some news about my job or just to say hello. There were many times I tried to look into the future and imagine how I would get through all those years filled with holidays and happiness, new babies and new homes, sickness and sorrow without my mother to lean on. As is almost always the case, we do get through. We get stronger, but it is not easy.

Imagine how overwhelming it must be for a young child to face life without a mother or father, to look down that long road of elementary school, high school, college, and beyond and see the empty space where a parent should be. There is a bond between most parents and children that runs far deeper than any other bond we encounter in our lifetimes.

For some children, the loss of a parent may not be the most difficult loss they will face. If a boy hasn't seen his father in six years, the father's death is going to have a very different impact than if his father had been living with him. By the same token, if a girl's grandfather was her main father figure, the death of her grandfather will be a monumental loss.

The same can hold true for aunts, uncles, cousins, friends, and teachers. Those who have key roles in a child's life, serving as mentors, friends, protectors, and surrogate parents, will be missed more deeply than those who have had only a passing acquaintance with the child. It is not always a matter of who was more loved but of who was more involved.

In most cases, losing a parent or a sibling will change the very fiber of a child's life. Mommy will no longer be there to walk him to school, to pack his favorite lunch, to tuck him in at night. In the case of a deceased sibling, the surviving child may mourn not only the loss of a sister, but also the loss of a roommate, a buddy, a sparring partner, and an ally. These losses cannot be stacked up and compared to the death of a grandparent who lives across the country or even a friend who lives down the street.

When it comes to dealing with children and their grief, all of the adults—those in helper roles as well as parents—have to try to resist the urge to think like adults. We need to get down on the child's level. Look at the death from a child's perspective. Think about the relationship the child had with the person who has died. Remember the way the death occurred and how that might be affecting this particular child. Then, in a sense, toss all of it out the window and simply listen to what he or she is saying and doing. That's where you'll find clues to what's going on inside and how you can make a difference.

Where does faith fit in?

For most of us, everything we think is true about life, death, and the afterlife is wrapped up in our religious beliefs. What we believe happens to us after we die can shape the way we react to death and the way we react to others in the same situation. Before we can begin to use our faith to guide children through grief and mourning, however, we must be clear and honest about our own feelings toward our faith and its teachings about death and resurrection.

If we are caught up in a blame game with God, accusing God of taking a loved one away as punishment for some action, it's entirely possible that we unwittingly pass on that view to a grieving child in our care. On the other hand, if we try too hard to sugarcoat the image of heaven and the concept of the afterlife, we could end up creating equally confusing and potentially damaging problems.

The Christian faith teaches that life never ends; it simply changes form. Often the death of a loved one can put that belief to the test, especially for children who may not have a full understanding of their faith just yet. It's up to us—teachers, chaplains, pastoral ministers, parents—to talk in an honest and simple way about our faith. In doing so, we can translate difficult concepts into meaningful lessons that will provide children with a road map of sorts through grief.

We cannot separate our faith from our grief and mourning. They are delicately intertwined, and for most of us, that is a blessing. Talk to people who have suffered tragic losses, and time and again they will say that they could not have made it through the difficult times had it not been for their faith. Even when they are angry at God and wondering about the wisdom of God's will, they are still connected to a powerful belief system that helps them make sense of the confusion.

I was a senior in high school when my grandmother was hit by a car while crossing a busy road in my hometown. We prayed to God, Mary, and every saint whose name had ever crossed our consciousness.

She died five years after the accident, having never recovered physically or mentally. At that point in my life, I was filled with faith. In fact, my mother and I had been returning from a youth group outing to see Pope John Paul II at Madison Square Garden in New York City on the day my grandmother was hit. Our bus passed the accident on the way back into town, but we had no idea how that scene would affect us. Throughout my grandmother's ordeal, I prayed. We all prayed, and we used our faith like a life preserver to keep us afloat in a stormy sea.

When my mother was diagnosed with cancer a few years later, I convinced myself that God would not take her. After all, he took my grandmother too young and too tragically. Surely he was not going to come knocking again at my family's door so soon. I'm not sure where that idea came from, thinking that God was keeping some kind of life-and-death tally. Maybe it was just a way to ward off the inevitable. The Sunday before my mother died was the first time in my life that I chose to skip Mass. I was trying to stare down God in a fight for my mother's life, and going to church while he let her die in our family room would have been like blinking first, or so I thought at the time.

When God—and death—did come for my mother early in the morning on April 12, I was not so filled with faith. I was filled with rage, disbelief, despair, and hopelessness. At that moment, faith seemed far out of reach.

Death forces us to look more closely at our faith and at how much we believe or don't believe. The night before my mother died, as we stood around her bed while our parish priest gave her the sacrament of the sick, my mother's father stood on the sidelines. He was adamant that she did not need the anointing, that she was going to be cured. He prayed his novena, not asking God to spare her life but asking that God's will be done. When my mother died the next morning, my grandfather did not lose faith. He may have been in anguish over his daughter's death, but he held fast to the belief that God does answer every prayer, just not always with the answer we want when we send up our request.

Where we are on our own faith journey will factor heavily into how we approach our grief journey and the way we deal with others who are on similar paths. Faith and grief almost seem to merge into one path. With wisdom and courage, the two parts can make us whole again. That wholeness will, in turn, make us better equipped to comfort and guide the grieving children who look to us for answers, acceptance, and understanding.

Grief and mourning—is there a difference?

What do those two terms—*grief* and *mourning*—mean, and how do they play out in everyday life after the loss of a loved one? Grief is the emotional stress caused by death or any other traumatic event. Mourning is the way we outwardly display that grief. While those definitions sound neat and clean, remember that when we're talking about our emotional lives, things are never that easy. Life is a roller coaster of feelings.

Every grieving child, regardless of age, and every grieving adult for that matter, must move through a series of stages known as tasks, as described by grief expert J. William Worden: We accept the reality of loss; we allow ourselves to feel the feelings that come with loss; we adjust to life without our loved one; and we invest in new relationships and move on with life.

The tasks represent our human response to grief and our effort to pull ourselves through it. They allow us to get through grief and mourning to a place where the loss we have suffered has been integrated into our lives in a healthy way. If we don't deal with issues that are simmering below the surface, we set the stage for potential problems that could linger for years. For children, getting caught in these unresolved tasks can spell developmental disaster that reaches well into adulthood.

In the chapters that follow, we will explore these four tasks in depth, looking at how they manifest in a child's life and how we can encourage children—whatever their ages or developmental stages—to work through each task. Together we will discover and discuss why kids need to grieve.

Talking about death

It can be hard for adults to watch a child deal with grief. We want the child to feel better, to return to "normal" as soon as possible. It helps if we can remember that when it comes to grieving, "normal" takes on a whole new meaning. Although every child and every loss is different, there are some basic guidelines for understanding and talking about death with a child.

Don't get into comparisons. One death is not worse than or better than another. Even the death of a goldfish can be a huge loss for a child.

Be compassionate and allow the child to feel sad or angry.

Don't be fooled by outward behavior. Children sometimes appear unaffected by loss, but in reality their grief will come out at some point. You can help it along by being available to a child in grief—to listen, to play, to cry, to pray.

Ask simple questions or make simple statements that help a child articulate his own feelings:

- "It sure is quiet around the house without Spot's barking. I miss him."
- "How are you feeling today? Do you want to go for a walk with me?"

- "This was Grandma's favorite [song, season, food, sweater, etc.]. Remember when [recall a specific event here]?"
- "Would you like to keep this [book, doll, necklace, etc.] as a reminder of your sister?"

Let a child see your own grief. If you are grieving too, don't be afraid to be sad together.

Say a favorite prayer together or make something up as you go along. You can use the reflection at the end of this chapter, "Healing the Hurt," as a guide.

Activity: From Caterpillar to Butterfly—Talking about Resurrection

It's hard for kids to grasp the concept of resurrection, so it helps if we can find a way to put this complex subject into simple terms. Here's one way to talk about resurrection with younger children.

Step 1. Read the storybook Waiting for Wings by Lois Ehlert (or some other butterfly book that may be a favorite of your child's). Talk about how the caterpillar was transformed into a butterfly after a short time in its cocoon. Reflect on the fact that the butterfly is not a different creature but the same caterpillar given a new kind of life. Help your child to see the original caterpillar in the transformed butterfly.

Step 2. Talk about how the transformation of our loved one from death to resurrection is similar to the caterpillar's transformation. When we die, we are transformed by God into new creations. We are the same but different. Just like the caterpillar, we are given a new life—eternity with God in heaven.

Step 3. Help your child create a caterpillar-butterfly to illustrate the concept:

- Take a cardboard tube from a roll of paper towels and paint it or cover it with contact paper or fabric. Add stickers, glitter, drawings, or any other designs.
- Take two pipe cleaners and glue them onto one end of the tube for antennae. Curl the ends up or glue small pom-poms to the ends. Now you have a caterpillar.
- Next, fold a piece of colored construction paper in half. Draw the outline of a wing on one half. Cut the folded paper so that when you open it the wings are symmetrical.
- Open the wings and let your child paint on one side only. Tell him to close the wings over and press the two sides together so that the painting creates a symmetrical design. Let the wings dry.
- Wrap the caterpillar in tissue, gauze, or even a towel. Explain to your child that the caterpillar is in its cocoon.
- The next day (or however long you'd like to wait—three days, perhaps), take the caterpillar out of its cocoon and glue it into the crease of the wings. The caterpillar has been transformed into a beautiful butterfly.

An alternative for older children:

Let older children or teens tap into activities or hobbies that make them feel comfortable. Technology might be one option. If a child uses a smartphone, tablet, or computer, invite her to explore this lifecycle theme—from caterpillar to butterfly, rebirth and resurrection—with visuals. Encourage her to find photos of butterflies and caterpillars, or, if she knows how to take photos, to capture her own images out in the yard or in a garden outside church or school. She could then intersperse these photos with pictures of her loved one, along with other photos that make her think of heaven and God and hopeful things, to create a digital slideshow or photo album. Similarly, a child could paint or draw or make a collage related to this same theme, if technology is too advanced or unavailable.

Questions for Reflection

» What is your first memory of death? How has that shaped your attitude toward loss, grief, and mourning?

» How prominently does your faith figure into your attitude toward and reaction to death?

» Can you identify instances when your own prejudices and experiences may have colored your response to someone who was grieving?

» Do you remember a time when you reacted in an unexpected way to a loss in your own life? Have you seen a child in your care react to death in ways that seemed inappropriate to you at the time? Reflecting back on that, what might have been at the heart of that behavior?

» How would you respond today if a child in your care came to you grieving the loss of a pet? A parent? A friend? A grandparent? Consider these scenarios ahead of time to lessen the fear factor.

Meditation: Healing the Hurt

Losing someone we love
is like losing a part of ourselves.
We feel an ache inside,
an emptiness that can't be filled.

Dear God,
give us the wisdom and grace
to recognize that ache
in the children we love and serve.
Help us say the right words,
do the right thing, as we
guide them on the path toward
healing and wholeness.

2
What Children Need to Know

- It may not look like grief
- Grasping the reality of death
- How much do children really understand?
- What does it mean when you die?
- Where to begin?
- Managing a first good-bye
- Answering common questions

Dying is nothing to fear. It can be the most wonderful experience of your life. It all depends on how you have lived.
—Elisabeth Kübler-Ross

Every so often and without warning, children will take you directly into the heart of darkness. One minute you're helping them with homework or out on a bike ride, and the next you're talking about death. It can be both frightening and breathtaking for parents and other adult helpers. You may be uncomfortable attempting to navigate this new and sorrow-tinged terrain, but at the same time you can't help but step back in awe and marvel at a child's often wise insights on this incredibly complicated subject. I've seen it again and again with my own children.

When my oldest child, now a young adult, was only two years old, we almost stepped on a tiny brown sparrow lying motionless on the sidewalk outside our favorite bookstore in Austin, Texas. We stopped, and Noah looked up at me with his big brown eyes as if to say, "Do something." I knelt down next to him and told him that the bird couldn't fly anymore, that his heart wasn't beating. He looked at me again and said, "The birdie's sleeping." I held his hand and, even though agreeing with his sleep theory would have provided a nice way out of a lot more questions and confusion, I told him, "No, the birdie is dead. He's not breathing. He's not going to wake up."

Later that night, when we were sitting around the dinner table, I asked Noah if he wanted to tell his father about his day. He reported on our trip to the bookstore and our discovery outside. Then he said quite matter-of-factly, "The birdie is sad." That was it. Somehow his two-year-old mind took what I was saying and translated it into something he could understand. No more flying, no more breathing, no more chirping. The birdie must be sad.

Fast forward to just a few years ago, when my youngest child, now eight, was only three years old. Chiara and I were picking Noah up from play practice at his Catholic school. She asked if we could walk through the church rather than around the outside. So we did, and in the darkened church we knelt down for a minute. I asked if she knew where Jesus was. She looked up at the crucifix over the altar, looked back at me and said, "Somebody's sad."

Coincidence? Not at all. This is how children try to wrap their tender hearts and minds around very big concepts. They find a place that feels familiar, something they can understand, and wait for us to respond. These are what we call "teachable moments," those everyday opportunities that allow us to delve into a sometimes-scary topic in a less-than-scary way. It is in these moments that we lay the groundwork for a healthy understanding of death and give our children the opportunity to prepare themselves for the bigger losses to come.

It may not look like grief

Children of different ages and developmental stages perceive death in different ways. A very young infant may sense on the most basic level only that something is upsetting his otherwise secure and happy environment. A teenager, on the other hand, may be overwhelmed by her understanding of the finality of death and her unwillingness to acknowledge her own mortality. Every age group in between has its own worries, confusions, beliefs, and reactions to losses that are suffered along the way—whether it's a family pet that is hit by a car, an older sibling who is killed in a tragic accident, or a beloved grandparent who finally succumbs to a hard-fought battle with disease.

If a parent is going through grief at the same time, he or she might struggle to understand a child's sometimes unusual way of assimilating sorrow and loss. A child may complain about having to miss an event because of the death or ask about the morbid physical details of burial or beg to go out for ice cream when everyone else wants to shut themselves away and cry. Children simply react from where they are at that moment in their development. Some will hit grief square on the head with "typical" or acceptable reactions and sadness, and others will come at it from what appear to be the strangest places. It's up to the adults around them to accept what they're saying in a nonjudgmental way, even if what we really want to do is correct or reprimand them or shake our heads in confusion.

In *Wish You Were Here: Travels Through Loss and Hope*, Catholic author Amy Welborn takes readers on a trip through Sicily with three of her five children in the aftermath of her husband Michael Dubriel's sudden death. She moves seamlessly from the winding, unknown roads of Italy to the winding, unknown roads of grief in a memoir that exposes the underbelly of loss in the most beautiful way.

Early on, Amy recalls how her husband used to have "Fun Fridays" with their two young boys. Only two weeks after his death, Amy had no plans to do Fun Friday because "the concept seemed not only absurd, but even disrespectful." Her boys, however, unaware of the "proper" way to grieve, had other ideas.

> But as they climbed out of the car that day, the decision happened, and I didn't make it. Joseph had connected some dots in his head. "Hey, it's Friday! Can we have Fun Friday?"
>
> *Fun Friday? What? Really?*
>
> We stood at the bottom of the stairs, they expectantly, me stunned. "Do you *want* to have Fun Friday?" I asked, carefully. Mostly for my own sake, carefully.
>
> "YES!" they shouted, and ran up the stairs ecstatic.
>
> I followed them slowly, confused. A half hour later we were at the wings place near our apartment, at their request, on that first Fun Friday without Mike. . . . The boys played on as they waited for their burgers. Sometimes, I admit, in those early weeks, I looked at them when they were grinning and laughing and I thought, *What is*

wrong with you . . . your daddy died. How can you live like this, here,
now? Don't you get it? Stop it . . . be sad.

I never said any such thing, of course. I just watched and tried
to learn.

Grasping the reality of death

Depending on a child's age, death can mean different things, making
the first "task" of grief somewhat complicated. As they journey
through the various stages of growing up, children learn to put abstract
ideas into a framework they can wrap their minds around. They use
the tools with which they are the most comfortable. For a very young
child, that may mean relying on the fantasy of fairy tales and cartoons
to explain the loss of a loved one. For a teen, it may mean withdraw-
ing even deeper inside himself in order to avoid the reality he knows is
out there.

Parents and other adults can reflect on where their children are in
these developmental stages before they start talking about death. How
do our children deal with other problems in their lives? Do they have
active imaginations that rely on magical ideas and fantastic stories? Are
they moving beyond those early coping methods to perhaps a more
realistic and concrete view of the world around them? Are they caught
between childhood and adulthood in the difficult teen years, where
they seem old enough to deal with adult concepts but in other ways
are not yet so grown up?

Often the best way to start this whole process is to sit back and listen to what children are saying. So often they lead us exactly where
they need us to be, if we are willing to open our ears and our hearts
to their ways of thinking and seeing. By listening and asking questions—not prying questions, but simple and direct questions—we can
learn exactly what our children need us to do for them.

In his book, *Helping Children Cope with Grief*, Dr. Alan Wolfelt states that listening to our children requires us to hear not only the content of what they are saying but also the many things they are only hinting at.

"Take your time and patiently listen to your child. If you expect yourself to comprehend instantly the total meaning of the child's communication and to heal immediately the child's grief, chances are that you will do a poor job of listening. If you find yourself being impatient in your effort to understand, you may unknowingly be treating the aftermath of the death in the child's life as an event rather than a process," he says.

Dr. Wolfelt explains that another indication that we adults may be trying to move children through the grief experience too quickly is our impulse to talk *at* children instead of listening to them. "Unfortunately, there are times when out of our sense of urgency to help the child we become more concerned with 'preaching' to the child than with listening and responding. Hopefully, we can recognize that we do not have to attempt to be all-wise and all-knowing to our children."

How much do children really understand?

For those who think babies, toddlers, and preschoolers are too young to understand that something terrible has happened, think again. Even the youngest children can sense when something is wrong in their families and their homes. They may not have the specifics, but they surely will know that you are upset and that something is threatening their routine.

Dr. Alan Greene, a California-based pediatrician who answers parents' questions on grief and other topics via his website, says that babies only hours old can pick up on a change in their parents' emotions. When mothers are grieving or depressed, children—from infants to teens—notice it and are affected by it. Their emotions, activities, and development can be shaped by the grief going on around and inside them.

"Kids are so wise about this stuff. They are extraordinarily emotionally perceptive, and when there is a loss in the family, even if it's somebody they don't know, they pick up on the grief of the others around them," Greene observes.

Dr. Greene explains that while kids are often more perceptive than adults at sensing what's happening emotionally, they are not good at articulating it or understanding it consciously. "It's something that impacts them. They react and respond to it, but they often are not able to say that they are grieving. That is true for infants who are not verbal but even for teens who are quite verbal but will often not make the connection between what's happening in their lives and the grief event that's going on," he says. "People want so much to shield kids from grief, but the truth is that once they have a loss, they will grieve for at least a year. To leave them alone in their grief is to isolate them, obviously the worst thing we can do for them."

As parents, we often feel uncomfortable bringing up the subject of grief or sharing our own pain with our children. We think they are too young to experience such heartache, but children will experience grief with or without our help. It's up to us as parents—or adults who work with or care for a grieving child—to get involved and let them know that it's OK to be sad and help them mourn in healthy ways. We just need to meet them where they are and try to understand the world from their points of view.

There are several developmental stages at which children have different views of death. One of the most crucial stages is what famed child psychological Jean Piaget classified as the "pre-operational stage," which is marked by magical thinking, egocentricity, and reversibility.

According to Linda Goldman, a Maryland-based behavioral therapist who specializes in grief counseling, at this stage, a five-year-old may know that his grandfather is buried in the ground but will still write a letter and expect a return letter back.

"Young kids also think that their wishes and thoughts make things happen. It's really marked by the five-year-old who says, 'I hate you. I wish you were dead.' The next morning the brother is killed. The five-year-old thinks that his words magically created that, and the words may haunt him through adulthood," she explains.

As children move beyond magical thinking, they enter what Piaget referred to as "concrete operation." At this point, children have a more realistic idea of age span. They're curious and want to know the facts about things, including death. An explanation that may have satisfied a five-year-old is no longer acceptable, and they begin to put together the bits and pieces of information until they fill in the whole story.

As children reach adolescence, any loss and grief they experience is compounded by the normal difficulties of being a teenager. They are already pulling away from their parents, seeking independence, and leaning more on their peers. When a death comes along, they often pull farther away, making it difficult or impossible for them to open up to anyone but a close friend.

Goldman notes that it helps for teens to have a peer support group. "Part of the teenage stage is self-absorption, being preoccupied with the present and thinking that they're invulnerable. They tend to look toward their peers for support. That's a key piece."

No matter their age, children will need to work their way through grief at their own pace. The loss they experience when they are five or thirteen or eighteen years old is likely to linger in their hearts and minds for years to come.

What does it mean when you die?

Jennifer Morgan remembers with vivid detail what it was like to learn that her fourteen-year-old brother had died. Although it was close to thirty years ago, the memories are still fresh. "I was ten years old when Robby died. He drowned on a Boy Scout trip. It was Memorial Day weekend. What a tragedy. I remember it like it was yesterday, him in the kitchen making potato pancakes, and I was on my way to a friend's birthday slumber party. He was leaving the next morning, and I kissed him good-bye. That was the last time I saw my big brother," Jennifer recalls.

She remembers being at the local ball park for a softball game when word came that there had been an accident. She and her younger brother and sister were taken to a friend's house. They waited there for hours before they were driven back to their own home, where friends and neighbors had gathered to comfort their parents.

"I walked in and saw my mom sitting in a chair crying. I was so confused. What happened? Our friend who is a priest approached us and said that Robby was in heaven. How could that be? I didn't get it. He was supposed to be in Delaware. From then on my life would never be the same."

So often we parents and other adults assume that children do not need to grieve. We try to protect them from the sadness and hurt. We send them away to stay with distant relatives. We ignore their questions in hopes that the curiosity will disappear on its own. Sometimes we even tell them stories that do more harm than good.

Like young Jennifer who could not understand how her brother could be in heaven when he was supposed to be in Delaware, children who lose a loved one must first come to understand the reality of what has happened before they can even begin to grieve. It is up to parents and other caring adults to help them make sense of the chaos and to give children the basic information they need to process the event.

"I remember telling the kids about Robby's death," says Lorraine Wilson, Jennifer's mother. "They related to heaven. They had a belief in God. We told them that Robby was not coming home. It was like telling a story. It didn't seem like we were telling them about our son, about Robby."

But telling them the truth was the best thing the Wilsons could do for their children. The reality was that Robby was never coming home, and if his siblings were going to accept that and begin to grieve and mourn, they had to know the truth.

We don't have to give children gory details of injuries and circumstances, unless they are old enough to ask about and absorb that information, and we shouldn't give them confusing euphemisms for death. We do have to give them the real story, even if it is an abridged version. According to experts, 99 percent of the time our children ultimately know the real story even when we think we are shielding them from it. Such efforts to veil or soften the truth serve only to break a trust between our children and the adults around them at a critical time in their lives.

In an article on the *New York Times* "Opinionator" blog, parent Abby Sher writes about her own death-denying mistakes when it came time to talk to her daughter about her deceased grandparents.

"I promised my five-year-old daughter, Sonya, that we could visit Grandma Joanie and Grandpa Roger 'soon.' This was impossible. My parents died before Sonya was born. But I didn't know how to tackle the what-happens-after-we-die talk, so whenever the subject of my parents came up, I had tried to divert her attention or say vague things like, 'They're very far away,'" she writes.

Sher recalls how the deaths of her aunt, father, and stepfather during a six-year span of her childhood left her confused, and when her mother used words such as "peaceful" and "a relief" to explain death, it only made matters worse. It's likely that those factors and her acknowledged lack of belief in life after death played into her willingness, or need, to skirt the issue of death when talking with her own child. Eventually, however, she had to confront the truth.

So the next Saturday morning, while our daughter was tracing hearts with her new markers, we had this conversation:

"Hey, remember when I said we could go visit Grandma Joanie and Grandpa Roger?"

"Yeah."

"Well, I was wrong. We actually can't. Because they died a long time ago."

Sonya laughed and said, "No they didn't!"

"Yes, they did," I continued. "And afterwards they became invisible, but we can think of them and look at their pictures. Some people say it's fun after we die and some people say it's quiet."

Sonya shrugged and went back to her artwork. Sher thought she had avoided the hard stuff, until they went to a party for a close family friend who had stage-4 cancer. Sonya's grief came out during the piñata festivities.

Sonya stamped her foot impatiently. She just wanted the candy to come down.

When we got home from the party, Sonya started pulling out the D word any chance she could.

Me: "Let's make a picture of our family."

Sonya: "But your family is DEAD."

Or Jay (waltzing with Sonya in his arms): "One day I'm gonna dance like this with you at your wedding."

Sonya: "Unless you DIE before then."

That little girl wasn't being a brat or rude or unkind, despite how it might sound. She was finally facing up to the grief that had been deferred and denied. We can lie, we can hide, and we can try as hard as we can to avoid the difficult conversations, but grief will find a way out one way or another.

So we start with honesty and move out from there. As is always the case, the best way to teach is by example. Children will learn how to grieve by watching the adults around them. We can sit down with a photo album of our loved one and talk about his favorite places, the things he said, the dreams he had. We can let our children see our own weaknesses and sadness in the face of sorrow, and, at the same time, our own strength and faith.

We can give children familiar and unintimidating ways to express what's going on inside them. If a child is up for it, encourage her to draw a picture or write a poem about what she is feeling. For those children who aren't ready to express themselves in such open and direct ways, we can offer opportunities to bare their souls through dolls and puppets or physical activity. Or when all else fails, a piñata full of candy.

Where to begin?

It is never easy to talk about death, especially when we don't *have* to, but there it is, always showing up when we least expect it. Sit down to watch just about any Disney movie with a child and you're likely to find yourself squirming through a heart-wrenching death scene. So many children's books, movies, fairy tales, and rhymes are filled with images of death, loss, and sadness. How do we explain the death of Bambi's mother? Should we even sing the "Rock-A-Bye Baby" lullaby with its boughs breaking and cradles falling? And don't get us started on Humpty Dumpty or the Three Little Pigs.

Most of us grew up on these favorites without a second thought to their deeper significance—that is, until we had children of our own and really started listening to the words. Should we ban all children's entertainment that includes death and sadness? No, says pediatrician Dr. Greene and other experts on childhood development.

"There is children's literature that does have death and renewal in it. Something like *The Lion King*, which is often disturbing for kids when they first see it, is a good kind of disturbing. It helps them deal with real events," he explains.

To this day I remember in vivid detail watching *The Land Before Time* with Noah when he was young. I was somewhat dumbfounded by the heartbreaking scene of the young dinosaur Little Foot and his dying mother and its presence in this movie for very young children. After his mother dies and Little Foot is left alone, he meets an older dinosaur, who listens to his sad tale. Little Foot blames himself, blames his mother, talks about his anger and his sick stomach. The older dinosaur nods knowingly and assures him that the stomachache will go away but the longing to see his mother again will stay for a very long time. Little Foot finds a "tree star" (a leaf) and keeps it with him as a reminder of his mother.

When the movie was over, I sat there expectantly, knowing my thoughtful and sensitive boy was not going to let that story line go unmentioned. Sure enough, we ended up in a difficult conversation about what happened to Little Foot's mommy and then, naturally, what happened to my mommy, who had died "a long time ago." It wasn't fun; it wasn't comfortable. And it forced me to walk that fine line between giving my son enough information and not scaring him with it. The discussion prompted further questions about other deaths: my friend, Bertha, whom he got to know before a heart attack took her far too early, and our dog, Chester, who died when Noah was only a year old. It was perfectly normal for Noah to want to understand the whats and whys of this thing called death. It also was perfectly normal for me to want to protect him from anything that might be more than he could handle—or more than he needed to know—at that moment.

For the longest time, I didn't tell my children that my mother was only forty-seven when she died. I shielded them from the reality that some moms die before they grow old. At the time, I was in my forties. Anyone who has ever lost a mother too young will tell you that your own life becomes a race against your mother's clock. Will I "outlive" her? Am I going to meet the same fate? What will it feel like to reach an age my mother never saw? If I had so many issues with my mother's premature death, how much worse would it be for my children to know that they, too, could be left motherless so soon?

Eventually, however, as each child got a bit older and was exposed more and more to a world where too many people die too young, I'd give them that detail. I'd watch them ruminate on it, turning it over in their minds and making calculations. It was as if I could see them doing the math behind their silent eyes. And more questions would follow.

We won't always have every answer, and maybe we'll even have to stumble our way through and make it up as we go, but in the end children are better off and better prepared for things that lie ahead because we took the time to answer their questions. Like the dead sparrow on the sidewalk, little everyday events that intrude into our lives and prompt children to ask questions remind us of the cycle of life that threads through our days, months, and years. From the dead spider on the kitchen floor to the leaves falling gently from the oak tree in the front yard, we are given ample opportunity to talk about birth, death, and rebirth.

Managing a first good-bye

Some farewells will be easier for our children to handle than others, and those are perfect opportunities to explore the subject and find those "teachable moments" we talked about earlier. When the pet goldfish dies, it's not silly to hold a memorial service, complete with eulogy and burial. (For more specific information on rituals and memorials, see chapter 9.) It may seem excessive to an adult, but to a child it is often a first glimpse of how we mark the passing of someone from one life to the next. It gives the child a chance to see that we honor the dead, celebrate their lives, and pray for them in the next life. We may be praying for Goldie the Goldfish today, but one day we will be praying for and saying good-bye to someone much dearer, and it will be easier because first we said a proper good-bye to Goldie.

In our family we have enjoyed the companionship of cats and dogs, hermit crabs and guppies, which means we have had pet funerals—quite a few of them, as a matter of fact. It's inevitable—and healthy. When our cat Hamlet died, we put his body in a cardboard box with a ball of yarn and some little treats, had a ceremony with the kids gathered around, and buried him in the backyard next to the spot where we had already buried our dog Greta's ashes. Our children cried, but it was the kind of crying that eventually brings relief and healing. They were sad to say good-bye to Hamlet and Greta and the fish that we buried rather than flushed, but when they go out to our backyard and see the stone markers near the St. Francis of Assisi statue where Greta and Hamlet are buried, or the rock at the foot of the Our Lady of Guadalupe statue where our fish are buried, they know that people and pets we love may die but their memories live on forever in our hearts.

Taking that to the next level, it can be helpful—wise, even—to allow a child to attend the funeral of a distant relative to help prepare him for the day he will be expected to do the same for a grandparent or parent or friend. Why take a child to a funeral unless absolutely necessary? Why bring a little one to a wake if he hardly knew this great-aunt or that elderly neighbor? Because it is absolutely necessary, at least if we want our child to face the difficult questions about death before they lose someone especially close to them. Children are so much more resilient than we like to believe. They tend to approach these moments more with curiosity than fear, especially if they are not in the throes of intense grief over a significant loss.

When my son was only three years old, we took him to the wake of my brother-in-law's grandmother. We opted to allow him to go up to the casket with us and ask questions. He wasn't scared or crying or even shy. He asked questions about her and about the box she was in. As he grew up, he attended the wake of a neighbor, a teacher, a friend's father, and a beloved parishioner. And when he was just shy of seventeen years old, he had to attend the wake and funeral of the first close relative, his great-grandmother, with whom he shared a birthday.

He and our other children were prepared for that moment because we had exposed them to the reality of death and, over the course of their lives, had talked about what we believe about the next life. When my grandmother was moved to a nursing home and began to deteriorate rapidly, I would talk to them about how she was ready to go on to the next part of her life, eternity in heaven. It was especially difficult for eight-year-old Chiara to grasp what I was saying, that I could want my grandmother to die. And so we took every opportunity to talk about what we believe and how my grandmother was no longer the same person and had said herself that she was "ready." Although her death was difficult and the children saw me cry, they also saw me stand at the casket and touch her forehead, laugh and smile with friends at the funeral home as we recalled some of her classic lines, and, finally, give the eulogy at her funeral. Sadness over our loss was balanced with a celebration of E-ma's life. Of course, mourning the death of someone who is just shy of 101 years old is a lot easier than many other losses that are sure to come their way, but without question our children have learned from the experience of their great-grandmother's life and death.

By inviting children to be involved in the lives of loved ones who are aging or dying and by allowing them to attend wakes and funerals for people they know—even distantly—we actually counter the normal fears that may creep up when we avoid the subject.

There is no easy way to avoid the hurt that comes with death, and so we have to learn to cope with it instead. We can become aware of our children's sensitivity to what is happening around them. People are crying; some may be angry. Dinner doesn't get made. The house is a mess. Mom doesn't ever seem to sleep. They will get caught up in all of it, and, if we don't talk to them, they will begin interpreting it for themselves, something that can be more frightening and more traumatic than hearing the truth. That's where we step in, take a deep breath, and begin the long grieving process by helping our children accept the reality and the finality of death, and our belief in eternal life.

Answering common questions

The question is not *if* a child will ask questions about death, but *when*. What follows below are some basic questions children may ask, depending on age, development, and how much they have been told up until that point. Use this Q&A as a guide rather than a script, adapting it to the child and situation. Some questions listed in the preschool section may be asked by elementary-age children or even teens. That's OK. There are no hard-and-fast rules when it comes to grief and how children will respond. Just listen to their questions and answer them as honestly as you can.

Toddler/Preschool Q&A

Q: What happens when you die?

A: Your heart stops beating. You stop breathing. Your skin loses its warmth. You don't feel anything anymore. You don't hear or talk. You don't think. You don't dream or wake up.

Q: Where do we go when we die?

A: We go to heaven to be with God. Even though our bodies don't work anymore, our souls—the part of us that makes us who we are—go to heaven and live forever. We believe that after we die we will be together in heaven with the people we love.

Q: Are you going to die some day? Am I going to die?

A: Everybody has to die, but we hope we will be around for a long, long time. Every person, every living thing, is born and lives and dies. It's part of life, and even though it's sad, God promises us that we can come and live with him when we're finished here on earth.

Elementary Age Q&A

Q: Why did Grandma have to die?

A: Grandma died from cancer, which is a very bad disease. Her doctors gave her medicine to try to make her better, but she was too sick. Her body was weak and couldn't keep working.

Q: I miss Spot. Why did he have to get hit by that car? I don't ever want another pet.

A: It's normal to feel that way. Spot was your buddy. He got out of the yard and ran into the street. It was an accident. I understand if you don't want to think about getting another pet. You can never replace Spot, and we wouldn't ever want to try. But maybe someday you'll find a puppy that needs a home, just like when you found Spot. For now, let's just remember Spot and how much we loved him and how happy he made us.

Q: What's going to happen to us now that Dad is gone?

A: We are going to be together. I will always take care of you and love you and protect you. I know it's hard to imagine life without Dad. It's going to be hard for me too. But we'll help each other through it, and we'll remember all the good times we had together. I'm here to listen any time you want to talk or ask questions or even if you just want a hug.

Q: I don't want to go back to school. What if the kids make fun of me because I don't have a mom anymore?

A: In a few days we'll go visit your teacher and the principal and talk about it. You do have to go back to school, and some kids might not know how to act, but it won't always be that way. As long as you let me know what's happening and what's on your mind, we can work through any problems together.

Q: Why did God take my sister away?

A: Sometimes bad things happen, and we don't understand the reasons. God doesn't take people to reward or punish them or us, but it still hurts. We have to remember that God is here for us when we're scared or upset, even when we are mad at God. It's OK to feel angry at God. Sometimes I feel angry with God, too, but we just have to remember that God loves us and will stay with us even when we can't feel God with us.

Teenage Q&A

Q: Why should I go to the wake and funeral? What difference will it make?

A: It's a time for us to get together with family and friends to remember Grandpa. It's a time to tell stories and share memories of someone we all loved. I know it won't be easy, but sometimes we have to do hard things for people we love, and we're better for it in the end. If you really don't think you can handle this, we can talk about what to do. Maybe you could stay in the back of the funeral home and not go up to the casket, or maybe you can just attend the funeral. A wake and funeral give us a really beautiful way to say one last good-bye. I would really love for you to be there with us, and I'll do anything I can to help you feel comfortable with it.

Q: How can I believe in a loving God when he could let my friend die?

A: Even though we believe in God and have faith, that doesn't mean it's easy. I know it's hard to understand how this could happen, but God didn't make it happen. It's normal to feel as if God let you down, though, and it's OK to get angry with God. Just try to lean on your friends and on us while you're going through this. And remember, you can still pray and talk to God about what you're feeling, even if what you're feeling is anger and confusion.

Q: Why do I feel so alone, even when my friends are around?

A: When someone we love dies, it sets us apart from other people. Friends might not know what to say or do when they see us. For someone who's never lost a loved one, it's not always easy to understand just how badly this hurts. Try to be patient with them, but in the meantime maybe we could find a grief support group for kids your age. I think it would help to talk about this with other people who have been through it.

Activity: Write a Letter

Writing a letter to a loved one may help your child figure out what he is feeling and why. Your child doesn't have to be a budding poet or novelist to put pen to paper. In fact, a nonreader could even dictate a letter to an adult or draw a picture that tells the story. Give your child the following instructions and then give him his space and privacy.

Step 1. Get a few sheets of stationery, a spiral-bound notebook, a fancy journal, even some plain old copy paper—whatever you like to work with best. Pick out a pencil or pen, crayons or markers, whatever you feel like writing with.

Step 2. Begin your letter as though you are writing a real letter to the person you love. If that's too difficult, write the letter to someone else who is close to you. No one else has to see this, so try to write whatever comes into your head, even if it sounds scary or like something other people wouldn't like. Just let your feelings come out on paper.

Step 3. Write about what you have been doing since you last saw your loved one. Have you been out much, keeping up with friends and hobbies, or going back to school? Do you have a hard time doing the things you used to do?

Step 4. Write about how you miss your loved one. Do you miss having someone to talk to, someone to kiss you goodnight, someone to walk with you to the bus stop, someone to eat lunch with at school? Just think about everything that has changed since your loved one died, and try to describe how that makes you feel.

Step 5. Describe what's going on around your house. How is your family doing? Are people acting differently? Are things very quiet? Very chaotic? Do they seem unchanged? How does all this make you feel?

Step 6. Once the letter is complete, put it somewhere special and reread it on your loved one's birthday or at holidays or on the anniversary of his or her death. It may help you see how you were feeling at the time and how you have progressed.

Adults can definitely consider doing this same exercise.

Questions for Reflection

» Are you hesitant to discuss death with your children? What makes it difficult for you? When was the last time you reflected on your own feelings about death and your experiences with grief?

» When you were a child, did you have any negative experiences related to death?

» When you were a child, were you included in wakes and funerals for loved ones, or did adults shield you from those events? How did that make you feel?

» Have your children asked questions about death, heaven, or life after death? How did you—or how would you—answer questions about those topics?

» Are there any losses in your life that still cause you pain, any unresolved grief or anger with God?

Meditation: Be Not Afraid

It's not easy to let go
of fear and sadness
when someone we love dies.
We want answers,
we want certainty,
we want comfort here and now.

Dear God, give us strength
to trust in your promises
and to walk in faith
even when we are afraid,
even when we cannot see
the path you have put before us.

3

Giving Children the Support They Need

- Normal reactions to death run the gamut
- Expect an emotional roller coaster
- Ages and stages influence understanding
- Begin with God
- Adult attitudes can help or hinder a child
- Working through anger

For what do you say to little children when they suffer a loss? Do you say, Well, that's it. Give up and give in. . . . No. You wouldn't ever want your children to respond to suffering that way, to even the most profound loss, to the greatest pain.

—Amy Welborn, *Wish You Were Here*

"I was mad because my mom didn't let me see my Aunt Irene before she died. She said I was too young, as if I would only remember the way she was right before she died. I could understand that if I was younger, but I was almost thirteen. So I was mad because I never got to say good-bye," relates Colleen Venne.

"When Mom didn't let me see Aunt Irene, I thought that maybe she didn't look like herself anymore. To me she always looked like Aunt Irene, even at the wake. But I was old enough to remember all the things we did together. I was always really close to her," she recalled. "After she died, I cried myself to sleep every night for two months. Nobody ever knew. I wrote a lot. I wrote in journals, and I wrote poetry. I made my confirmation just a couple of weeks after she died. Picking her name for my confirmation name was like keeping her with me. I still go to the cemetery all the time and talk to her. Whenever I'm debating something or unsure about something, I go to the cemetery and ask myself, *What would Aunt Irene say?*"

What Colleen experienced as a child is nothing unusual. Confusion, anger, sadness, guilt, and fear come with the territory when someone we love dies. For children, those feelings can be compounded by the fact that they are often isolated from the adults around them, especially during the first days of deep grief and mourning. Perhaps a child is sent to the home of a friend during the wake and attends only the funeral. Maybe she's allowed to attend the wake but is told to sit at the back of the room and not approach the casket. So often parents think that death is too scary for their children to confront in such a direct and sometimes difficult way, but this is not the time to cut children out of the loop. It's precisely the time for parents and other adults to ask children about their feelings, to watch for both verbal and nonverbal messages they might be sending out, and to walk beside them as they experience some of these emotions for the first time.

As children begin the second task of grieving—allowing themselves to feel the many feelings that come with loss, it's healthy and necessary for them to experience the powerful emotions of grief with their whole beings. They need to find ways—or be given ways—to cope with those feelings and how they are playing out. They may be scared by their own anger. They may be overcome with fear. They may be drawn so deep into sadness that they pull away from their family and friends and the world around them. Caring adults can help ease the pain by letting children know that it's OK to have those sometimes-frightening feelings. How do we do that? It's as simple as making yourself available—physically and emotionally—to a child in grief, offering to listen, to talk, or just be a comforting presence until the child is ready to explore and express his feelings more deeply.

Normal reactions to death run the gamut

As our children go through the early stages of grief, there will be some pretty typical outward signs of the emotional battle raging within. It is completely normal for a child to experience any or all of the following symptoms:

- Sleep disturbances
- Changes in appetite
- Headaches
- Stomach pain
- Regressive behavior

- Increased fears
- Anger
- Guilt
- Acting out in school
- Disinterest in school, sports, music lessons, etc.
- Concern about his own health or that of his parents, siblings, etc.

When these behavior changes continue for an extended period of time or intensify to the extent that a child is unable to function at home or in school, you may need to seek outside help. Any signs of serious depression, any suicidal comments, or any signs of alcohol and drug abuse or violence indicate a need for immediate help.

Pediatrician Alan Greene says that aggression is a very common way for kids to grieve. They may begin bullying others or allowing themselves to be bullied. "Inability to pay attention, ADD/ADHD symptoms, school performance dropping off—all of that is common, depending on the age level of the kids. Temper tantrums are very common in children up to four or five years old as part of grieving."

Parents can share concerns about a child's grief symptoms with their pediatrician. Because the pediatrician may already be aware of that child's temperament, existing health problems, and religious and cultural background, she may be in the perfect position to watch for warning signs that require outside help and to advise family members on how to cope.

If you are an adult helper and you notice warning signs or other worrisome behavior, try to find out—in a sensitive and delicate way—if something is happening in the child's life that might be triggering the problems. While you as an adult helper may be well aware of any major losses in a child's life (parent, sibling, grandparent), you may not get the same information for losses considered "minor" (a distant relative, the grandparent of a friend, even a pet hamster or fish). And yet every loss, even those that seem far removed from a child's day-to-day life, can have dramatic and unexpected impact.

Expect an emotional roller coaster

Whether children are toddlers, teens, or anywhere in between, they will be hit full force during the grieving process by an array of emotions that may take parents—and the children themselves—by surprise. Especially for very young children, these may be feelings they have never experienced before. They will look to the adults around them for confirmation that it's OK to let out those feelings. If we don't allow children to express their feelings of grief, those pent-up emotions may block them—academically, socially, intellectually, and spiritually—and prevent them from experiencing life fully later on.

Donna Schuurman, executive director of the Dougy Center in Portland, Oregon, says that the children who end up at her grief center often demonstrate behaviors that other people don't understand. They act distracted, skip homework, get into fights, lie, sleep more than usual, and disobey the rules in general. A lot of parents don't know how to react when their children stop talking to them or start "acting out." This term should be struck from the bereavement vocabulary, according to Schuurman, since such behavior is, in reality, a cry for help that could save a child.

"Children act out the pain that's inside of them, and that's a good thing," she explains. "If we don't attend to them, they're going to have to keep making their actions louder and louder so that people won't keep missing them. What frequently happens is that people just slough it off, telling themselves that the child is just trying to get attention. Yes, they are trying to get attention, and if they don't get it, they're just going to have to keep doing more and more radical things."

The behavior of the kids who seek support at the Dougy Center is all over the map, from setting fires to becoming completely truant. Schuurman recalls one girl who had been a straight-A student and a high-school cheerleader until her boyfriend shot and killed himself in front of her because she was going to break up with him. In her shock, she ran—still covered in blood—to the local mall in search of a friend. Around school, however, the story deteriorated quickly, and she was cast as a selfish person who decided to go shopping after witnessing her boyfriend's suicide. It wasn't long before she stopped going to school and even stopped going home.

"Every other Thursday this girl would show up at the Dougy Center. Nobody was making her come here. She would just come and sit in the opening circle, and very often she would fall asleep. That was how she worked on her grief. Our center was a safe place to come and sleep," Schuurman adds. "She's now in college. I shudder to think what would have happened if we had said, 'You can't come here and sleep.' So our process is very much geared toward trusting that by providing a safe place and acceptance, children and adults will do the grief work that they need to do."

Let's discuss further a few of the emotions that may show up in children's behavior.

Anger. Name the emotions that first come to mind when you talk about a loved one's death, and anger will be at the top of the list. Children may be overcome by anger—with themselves, with their parents, with God—and that can affect their lives in powerful ways. Adults can watch for signs of that anger, such as a sudden urge to hit or throw things, a particular tone of voice, or even silence that is uncharacteristic of the child.

Gregory Floyd's young sons David and John Paul were hit by a car while playing outside their home in New Jersey. David survived; John Paul did not. David went to his father one day and said that he was a "teeny bit angry" with the man who hit them. Gregory used that moment of honesty to begin a conversation about feelings of anger and the idea of forgiveness.

"You don't want to talk about it prematurely. You want to validate their feelings. You want to say, 'Hey, this is very real for you to feel angry, and I'm not surprised. I'm not alarmed. I understand. I'm angry too, and it's a perfectly appropriate response to having life snatched away from you, but you don't want to stay there.' I told him that anger can be a cage that we get imprisoned in. Then we talked about forgiveness."

Lorraine Wilson, whose fourteen-year-old son Robby drowned on a Boy Scout outing, recalls how her young children reacted to their brother's death. "When the kids were younger, the biggest personality change I saw was in Peter (who was six when Robby died). He had always been such a gentle, happy little boy. He became very angry. He would hit me and tell me he hated me."

Anger is often a child's way of dealing with frustration, sorrow, pain, and confusion. It may not be easy to handle or pleasant to watch, but it is necessary for healing. Most of us, especially if we're parents, have been on the receiving end of a child's anger at one time or another, even after a minor incident. Reach back and remember how you dealt with that anger in a positive way, or perhaps reflect on the way someone helped you through your own anger over some traumatic incident, and use your firsthand knowledge to deal with the grief-related anger you may be witnessing now. It's critical that you avoid making children think that their anger is bad; anger they hide now will lead to serious problems later.

Fear and Separation Anxiety. When Kathy Duke's four-year-old daughter, Emma, died of cancer, one of Kathy's first concerns was her son Joseph, who was just shy of his sixth birthday. Although Joe had been included in Emma's sickness and treatment from the very beginning, learning to cope without his sibling was another story. The Dukes called on a local hospice organization and joined a grief support group.

"The first three or four meetings, whenever they started talking about their feelings Joe would get up and walk away," says Kathy. "Finally one time he was there with just the counselor. He was asked to help set up. After that time, he felt that he was an integral part of the thing. He really opened up."

Joe was reacting in ways that are typical of children who lose a loved one. "He started having nightmares," Kathy explains. "The counselors told us that this was actually a positive and healthy thing because it meant that he was dealing with it on a certain level."

One of the most difficult parts of her son's grief was that he became so fearful. "He was devastated when Emma died. He had become quite independent, but after she died he wanted to stay right by us. He didn't want to go into another room without us. If my husband was five minutes late coming home, Joseph would just cry and cry and say, 'Daddy's been killed in a wreck.' If I had any piece of advice for other parents it would be to include the children as much as you possibly can. Be open to their feelings and what they're saying."

Guilt. One of the most common reactions kids have to death is guilt. Even if the death is the result of something they couldn't have had any control over, they often feel responsible when someone close to them dies.

Colleen Venne, who talked earlier in this chapter about her anger after missing the chance to say good-bye to her dying aunt, experienced her own misplaced guilt after her grandmother was hit by a car years earlier.

"I was nine when Nani died," recalls Colleen, now forty. "I blamed myself. Until I was in my twenties I thought that she had been coming to our house to watch me the day she was hit. I never knew that she wasn't, so up until then I thought it was my fault. I blamed myself the whole time."

Once again, Colleen's reaction is completely normal. Her feelings of guilt were real, even though her mother, Margaret Robertson, says she has no recollection of any specific comments or events that might have triggered those feelings in her daughter. Children can create guilt where none exists. It's just another way they deal with the difficult circumstances of grieving.

Relief. Although it may be shocking to consider, sometimes children feel relieved when a loved one dies. Some circumstances surrounding what can be an unsettling reaction are obvious: long illness, pain, suffering, a loved one who no longer looks or acts the way he used to. For many children, death is a relief. That's not an easy thing to admit, so it's an especially troubling emotion for kids to negotiate, and it usually goes hand in hand with guilt.

There are other, more problematic reasons a child might feel relief at someone's death. If that person was abusive toward the child, or if the child witnessed that person hurting himself or others, relief can be a natural response now that this person is gone. Whatever the reason, children absolutely need help working through this complicated grief. First and foremost, they need to understand that those feelings do not make them bad people. There can be no judgment here. Every feeling is a legitimate feeling once children are plunged headlong into the world of grief and mourning, sometimes long before they are mentally and emotionally prepared to deal with death and loss.

Ages and stages influence understanding

Children of every age will react to death in unique ways, depending on their age. But how do we explain death to a child who cannot yet express his feelings verbally? How can we help a child accept a tragedy that is almost entirely beyond her comprehension, maybe entirely beyond our own comprehension as well? As adult caregivers we have to rely on our innate sense of what children need, whether it's the parental instinct that makes you know without question that your child is sneaking a cookie before dinner or that teacher instinct that allows you to sense when a child is saying one thing but meaning something completely different. We can be prepared, even if we can't anticipate every question or problem.

Babies. Babies will pick up on the tension in their environments and may even sense the stress in the arms of the people who are holding them. They will react to a parent's or sibling's tears or anger. Although they do not yet walk or talk, they do feel.

A baby may simply need to be kept in some semblance of a normal routine—naps at nap time, dinner at 6:00 p.m., bed-time lullaby, and good-night. But keeping a normal routine can be difficult for a parent who is grieving. You may need to enlist the help of a relative or friend who is close to your child. Ask a friend to come over and play with your toddler every afternoon before nap time. See if a nearby relative is willing to visit every morning to get breakfast on the table and get the little ones dressed. It may sound like a lot to ask, but most friends are happy to help in a time of crisis or need.

Teachers and other caregivers, too, can aid parents by helping children keep their routines at school or day care. The normal rhythm of life at school or at the babysitter's house will be a comfort to children whose home life may be in upheaval or total shutdown.

Preschoolers. Young children experiencing grief may become clingier or may develop a fear of the dark. They may begin wetting the bed, eating differently, or wanting to sleep with parents. Such changes in behavior may be due, in large part, to their fear of what they don't understand. Our job as their adult caregivers is to pay attention, offer a lot of reassurance, and keep the lines of communication open. We can begin by explaining some of the things that are probably most confusing to a three- or four-year-old.

Peggy Bohme, one of the founders of the Warm Place, a grief support center in Fort Worth, Texas, says that parents and other adult caregivers can help preschoolers in grief first by giving them the very basics about what it means to be dead: You don't move; you don't breathe; you don't feel or hear anything; you don't eat or go to the bathroom. She lets the children use a stethoscope to listen first to a sidewalk and then to somebody's heart.

"Just telling them what is alive and what is dead is a big part of what needs to be done," Bohme observes. "And feelings are important. What is a happy feeling and what is a sad feeling? We help them put words to those feelings."

When my son, Noah, was still a preschooler, I remember him doing exactly what Peggy explained. He used simple emotional terms to understand a complex concept. When he was three, he asked about the photograph of my mother that sat on the bookcase in our living room. I explained that he didn't know this grandma because she died a long time ago. He put down his snack and with a look of confusion said, "But she looks happy in the picture." She was smiling, so how could she be dead, which in his mind equaled sad?

That's how preschoolers operate. They call on simple emotions they understand—happy, sad, mad, scared—to explain more difficult subjects. But simplifying things doesn't necessarily clear up their confusion.

Gregory Floyd's daughter Rose, who was four when her brother John Paul died, came down to breakfast the day after his funeral and asked, "Where's Johnny?"

"That just threw us across the room mentally. You wonder, *How could she not get this?* We weren't mad at her, but it was simply amazing," Gregory says. "She watched his coffin go into the ground yesterday, and she's wondering where he is. I think that is the mercy of God because I think the Lord draws a veil and lifts that veil a bit at a time according to what the children are intellectually and emotionally capable of dealing with."

Elementary School Kids. As children move out of the preschool stage and into the elementary school age, their feelings of grief begin to change, with heavy emphasis on magical thinking during the early elementary years. For instance, if a child had ever wished a person dead, and that person does die, the child will think that the death is his fault. And even if he understands on some level that dead means gone forever, he still expects the person to return.

If you think back to some of your favorite fairy tales and cartoons, you'll have some idea of what's going through a child's mind at this age. Snow White and Sleeping Beauty come back from deathlike states. Road Runner and Wile E. Coyote, Tom and Jerry, Elmer Fudd and Daffy Duck—none of them ever succumbs to the things that would kill a real person. Kids at this stage are on that wavelength. Death is reversible to them. It's forever, but what does forever mean to an eight-year-old?

Young children often cannot sit down and explain how they feel, but there are other ways to help them express their fears, confusion, and anger. Give them crayons and ask them to draw, or take them outside and let them run off steam. Grief is not the time to ask children to sit quietly and avoid play and laughter. In fact, it is often through playing and acting "normal" that they protect themselves from the shock of death and begin to process the information in ways they can handle. Let them kick a ball around the yard or pound a piece of clay. Think of how nice it would be if we adults could do the same when the pressure of grief gets to be too much for us.

Lorraine Wilson took her three children with her to meetings of the Compassionate Friends, a grief support organization. There the children would draw pictures that gave her insights into what they were thinking. "The kids knew Robby wanted to fly, so one of them drew a picture of him in an airplane. He said, 'Here I am flying in Robby's airplane. I don't want to come down.' That's how they would express their feelings."

Older children may prefer to write down their feelings in a journal or ask questions of their parents, clergy, or other close adults. They may want to help plan the funeral or participate in the funeral Mass or memorial service. But first they need to be invited. Elementary-age children as well as pre-adolescents need to know that their questions and their presence are welcome.

Teenagers. Teenagers may react to grief by not seeming to react at all. They may appear disinterested, as if the death has not affected their day-to-day lives. Over time, however, that reaction begins to wear thin and other signs of unprocessed grief begin to surface.

Although teens in grief may experience many of the same physical symptoms as younger children, their reactions might surface in stronger, more dangerous doses. What may be a temporary decrease in appetite for a preschooler can become a full-blown eating disorder for a teen. An increased tendency to pick schoolyard fights for an eight-year-old can turn into a violent streak in a teen that makes him a danger to himself or others. Of course those are the extremes, but any of the following symptoms can be early warning signs that outside help is necessary:

- Aggression—picking fights, hitting or kicking, setting fires, throwing things, speaking in violent terms
- Complete withdrawal from family life—isolation, disinterest in life in general, complete silence, eating or sleeping disturbances that have the potential to create health problems

- Refusal to go to school, refusal to participate in the usual activities
- Fears that interfere with normal activities, such as sleep, meals, school, play
- Regressive behaviors that go on for an extended period—thumb sucking, bed-wetting, sleeping with parents, baby talk in younger children
- Lying to parents, teachers, friends
- Depression
- Indifference or denial that never progresses to expressions of grief
- Alcohol and drug use or sexual promiscuity in older children
- Suicidal thoughts or actions—talking about suicide, giving away personal belongings, any sign that a child is desperately seeking attention or help

While some of these symptoms can be found in any teen going through a difficult adolescence, all of them can be directly related to grief. The last three—alcohol and drug use, sexual promiscuity, and suicidal tendencies—should prompt immediate action and a call to a healthcare professional who is trained to deal with such behavior. Don't wait out those kinds of behaviors, thinking it's just a typical teenage phase. Take any serious warning sign as just that, a warning and a cry for help, and act swiftly.

The majority of teens will go through some form of the less severe symptoms without getting pulled down into dangerous terrain. The key, experts say, is for parents and other adults to pay attention to what they are doing or saying, especially anything out of character. Any sudden or profound transformation in behavior, attitude, or physical appearance is a sign that a child is struggling with something deeper.

Teens may have many questions but won't necessarily want to ask their parents or other adults. Often they will pull away from their families and rely on the support of their peers. A lack of emotion and a reliance on friends are typical of teens caught in the tug-of-war between childhood and adulthood.

Those of us who are the adults in their lives can make them feel safe and leave the door to communication open by being available to them while making sure we don't judge or yell, push or ignore. It's a delicate balance, but if we take our cues from the young people themselves, they're likely to show us exactly what they need even if they don't want to sit down and have a heart-to-heart talk.

Begin with God

Thomas Kane, principal of St. Thomas the Apostle School in Delmar, New York, has had to deal with his share of grief and mourning in his small suburban school. He has seen up close the way sorrow and loss can affect teachers and students alike: a soccer coach died on the field in front of students; a much-loved parent died of colon cancer; a first-grader had to cope with the death of a grandfather. The repercussions of these events are inevitable and fraught with doubt and confusion, even in a faith-focused environment.

"I do my best to begin with God. That's not always easy, even in a community of faith. As much as we want to have a strong faith, it is frequently during this time of grief that our faith is shaken," he notes. "It's a very difficult time. The words we choose to use or not use, the way we carry ourselves, and the way we try to reach out to hold onto something comforting are all part of the process. God is there all along; we just need to reach out and welcome his healing grace. Easier said than done."

When it comes to helping his students deal with grief, Tom takes his lead from the children themselves. Stories, images, and metaphors are especially helpful in giving children an age-appropriate and manageable way to cope with death, even if those metaphors might not feel right for adults. If a child needs to view a deceased relative as "up in heaven" watching over him, that's fine, he says. They will grow into a more mature view of life and death and faith in their own time. Tom believes that "above all else, children want to know that everything is going to be all right." He saw this truth when he had to substitute teach in a first-grade classroom.

He had no idea at the time, but one of the six-year-old students was in the process of losing a grandparent. The death was getting closer, and, as Tom learned later, the child was really grief stricken. Tom's lesson on Jesus' death and resurrection became a turning point in this child's process of letting go of his grandparent without fear, even though he would continue to feel sad.

"We spoke of the boundless love that we believe surrounds us in God's kingdom and how when we die, we are 'welcomed home' by God. The child's parent e-mailed me the next day and thanked me for talking to her child. She said my words helped her son see that death is a part of life; he said to her that night that Gammy was going to be OK when she died," Tom explained.

"This was an unplanned lesson. It was an unexpected absence for the teacher, and I had no choice but to fill in at the last minute. However . . . I learned a very important lesson about teaching children about death," he added. "They need to know what it means. Children need to be aware of what our faith traditions and teachings have to say about everlasting life. Our culture uses images of death and mourning that belie the truth of salvation."

Adult attitudes can help or hinder a child

Probably one of the hardest realities for the adults, especially parents, in a child's life, is that we cannot take away a child's grief. There's a sense of helplessness when we know a child is hurting, aching, longing for someone, and we cannot fill the void. If we happen to be grieving ourselves, the process is even more painful. We don't have the energy; we don't have the objective perspective; we don't have the physical or emotional ability to pull ourselves out of our own pain to see our children's grief in a clear and distinct way.

Remember Colleen Venne from the beginning of this chapter? Her missed opportunity to say one last good-bye before her aunt's death has stayed with her into adulthood, but it had its beginnings in her own mother's grief.

Her mother, Margaret Robertson, can remember in vivid detail the night Colleen wanted to see her dying aunt. Margaret's sister, Irene, was lying in a bed in the family room fighting to stay alive. Her cancer had progressed so far in those final days that she was unable to walk or eat or even hold a conversation. Margaret says that the main reason she did not bring her daughter for a visit was that she did not believe her sister was that close to death. She was hoping for a miracle, or at least for a few more days. She never imagined death would come so quickly.

Without a doubt, our own grief or view of death affects the children in our care. As the grown-ups in a situation, we can be examples of healthy grieving by sharing our feelings and letting children know that we're hurting too. Although children like to believe adults have all the answers, sometimes it's good for them to see us struggling alongside them.

Despite our best efforts to talk and listen, sometimes the children in our care are going to need more help than we can give them. If they demonstrate behaviors that cause concern, there are a mulititude of ways to help: counselors who specialize in grief or child development; grief support programs specifically for children; art therapy programs;

church-sponsored bereavement programs; clergy counseling; and close relatives and friends (see referrals in "Resources for Healing").

When we start worrying that a child is not reacting appropriately, we can stop and think back to little Joseph Duke, whose nightmares were actually positive signs and whose initial fears and anxieties were part of healthy grieving. Children react differently to death than adults do. Although they may want to play baseball in the middle of a memorial service, they are hurting on the inside. Play and laughter are ways they can escape the grief, if only for a moment, and gather strength for the rest of the process.

Peggy Bohme compares children in grief to a ball being pushed under water: no matter how hard you push it down, it pops back up again. "Children will grieve intently and then come up for air," she observes. "They can absorb only so much and then they need to play baseball or go to a movie or sit and do their homework."

It's important to let grieving children know they are not bad or strange because of how they feel. Tell them it's OK to play and laugh and work and cry. As parents and adult caregivers we can sit back and let children show us what they need—whether it's a trip to the ice cream parlor or a late-night talk at the kitchen table.

Working through anger

Every child gets angry. Sometimes it's over something no more serious than a broken toy; other times it is over the devastation of a broken heart. Here are some additional tips for helping a child work through anger:

- Acknowledge the anger and resist the impulse to squelch it. Your child needs to express these feelings or they will build up under the surface.

- Let your child know it's normal to feel angry under the circumstances.

- Share your own experiences with similar anger. Maybe you were mad one time because someone you loved died (or moved away, or became ill). Let your child know that you understand these feelings.

- Try to help your child move past the anger. Ask what's making her mad—that Mom didn't fight harder to get well, that Dad won't be here to coach Little League anymore, that Grandma won't be around to read stories and go for walks, that Spot won't be there to sleep on the end of the bed.

- If your child expresses anger toward God, let him know that's OK. Then try to talk about God, that God doesn't "take" people away from us, and that we can turn to God even in our anger.

Activity: Anger Buster

Use the following activity to help a child get feelings of anger out in the open. Don't be afraid to alter the activity to better suit a particular child's personality, needs, or abilities.

Step 1. Take a moment to talk about your deceased loved one with your child.

Step 2. Give your child a lump of modeling clay or Play-Doh and table space to work.

Step 3. Turn on some dramatic music (classical or whatever best suits you and your child).

Step 4. Let your child pound the clay to the beat of the music.

Step 5. Allow your child to pound, stretch, roll, and tear the clay in order to let out pent-up feelings in an acceptable way. (This may also give you some insight into the way your child is really feeling.)

Step 6. Experiment with different kinds of music in different environments.

Step 7. Feel free to grab a piece of clay and join in. You may be surprised at how much it helps.

Don't limit this exercise to a one-time event. Use it whenever there's a lot of tension in the air. Remember that this activity is not supposed to be a chore. It should be healing, expressive, and most of all, fun. It's also good for children of all ages. Even teens can benefit from a little stress-relief via a lump of clay, even if it's just kneading and molding the clay or creating something with it. Clay is an equal-opportunity medium.

You don't have to limit yourself and your child to clay pounding. Expand this music-based activity to include other art forms, such as painting or dancing, if that betters suits your child.

Questions for Reflection

» What, if any, worrisome behaviors are you noticing in your child or a child in your care?

» Think back to when you were your child's age. Do you remember feelings of fear, rage, confusion, or sadness? What caused those feelings?

» How did the adults in your life help you deal with those feelings? How can you use your own experiences—for better or for worse—to help shape the way you guide your child through grief and mourning?

» Have you thought at any point that you might need outside support to help you deal with your child's feelings and behaviors? What made you feel that way? What if you made one call today—to a friend, a clergy member, a counselor, a bereavement support group—to get some assistance? Would that help you feel less alone?

» Are there other adults in your child's life who could be ready helpers? Teachers, coaches, babysitters, day care workers, anyone who spends significant time with your child needs to be in the loop. Have you spoken to them about what you and your child are experiencing? If not, can you set a time to do so?

Meditation: Truth Conquers Fear

We search for words,
we search for meaning,
as we face the questions
that death stirs up
in our own hearts, in others,
in children who are dear to us.
We ask you, Holy Spirit,
to strengthen our spirits
so that we may guide these little ones
through the darkness of death
into the light of your love,
a love that answers every question,
calms every fear, heals every heart.

4

Helping Children Adjust to Permanent Loss

- Adapting and adjusting to a new reality
- Where and how do we begin?
- Obstacles to healthy adjustment
- Grief has no set timetable

> *The experience of loss does not wait for children*
> *to grow into adulthood.*
> —Alan Wolfelt, *Helping Children Cope with Grief*

Death never seems to come at the right time. It shows up when a son is preparing to graduate, when a daughter is about to get married, when a first communion is around the corner, when a family has just moved to a new home far from everyone they know and love. It catches us off guard. Even when everyone thinks we should be ready to handle it, even when *we* think we should be ready to handle it, death shows us how very little we know about the ins and outs of sorrow.

Suddenly we find ourselves—or our child or someone else we love—acting in ways we couldn't have predicted just weeks or days before. We don't recognize ourselves. We need someone who really loves us to meet us where we are and help us get to where we need to go.

My brother Fred was eighteen when our mother began the final days of her fight with colon cancer. As she slipped into a coma, Fred acted as though nothing in his life was changing. He stayed in his room with the television on while the rest of us kept vigil around our mother's bed. He went out with his girlfriend on dates while we cried over what we knew was surely the end.

On our mother's final night, Fred was up in his room as usual. Although the rest of us were keenly aware that my mother might not live until morning, Fred had yet to visit her bedside in the family room for one last good-bye. Finally, I went up to his bedroom, knocked on the door, and told him point blank what he had been trying to avoid: Our mother was dying, and if he did not say good-bye now, he would never again have the chance.

Fred came into the family room, walked over to a corner, slumped down onto the floor, and began to cry. He slept with the rest of the family on the floor that night. He was there when our mother came out of her coma at 5:00 a.m. that April morning for one last glimpse of her family and a final few, struggling breaths.

The months that followed were particularly hard on Fred, who was due to graduate from high school in June. Suddenly sports, proms, and parties weren't important. He gave up playing baseball. He went through the motions of graduation with our father alongside him and me in our mother's place at the ceremony.

Not long after, I moved across the country, causing Fred to suffer a second—although much less significant—loss. A year later our father remarried, and soon after that our sister, Tricia, followed me to Texas. For Fred it was like experiencing abandonment and loss over and over again. It made it hard for him to adjust to his initial and overwhelming grief over our mother's death. It would have been hard for anyone to adjust to that much change in such a short time, but being a teenager on the verge of adulthood made it that much harder.

Fred's behavior during our mother's death and his subsequent difficulty with the grief that followed provide a textbook example of what teenagers do when they must deal with the death of a close relative or friend. They withdraw, pretend they are not affected, and act as though death cannot touch them, even when it is just down the hall.

Those feelings of immortality and that attitude of disinterest can carry them through the early days or months of grief, but eventually they realize they must grieve. They have to find a way to learn how to live within a new kind of framework.

That is what this third task of grieving is about: helping kids learn to live without their deceased loved ones. We can foster this through rituals and commemorations that keep the person's memory alive. We can light a candle or write a poem. We can share stories about a loved one. We can try to avoid additional stresses that may compound a child's grief. This phase of grief is not about learning to forget but about learning to remember in a balanced, healthy way.

My best friend, Robin Gerrow, remembers how her ten-year-old son, Nathan Rhodes, reacted to their elderly dog's death. "We really didn't have any kind of ceremony when Grendel died. Nathan took it a lot harder than I expected. I didn't think he even liked the dog very much. He knew Grendel was sick but was still surprised at his death. The day he died, we made a point of having dinner together—a rare occasion—and telling our favorite stories about him. We laughed a lot and cried even more, but I think it was helpful that Nathan saw that we could do both at the same time. We could remember the good times and the times that Grendel was a real pain, and still love and miss him."

That's a key piece of information for parents and adult helpers: We can show children how to grieve by opening ourselves up to them. We cannot expect them to sit down and pour out their hearts if ours are closed off. They need to see that we are human, too, that we cry and laugh, get angry and sad. They need to know we will not cast a disapproving eye if they need to express their grief in front of us.

Adapting and adjusting to a new reality

Children, regardless of age or developmental stage, need to learn how to adjust to the new circumstances of their lives if they are going to work through their grief and emerge healthy and whole. Sometimes that will be a monumental task, as in the case of adjusting to life without a mother or father. Other times it will be difficult but manageable, such as when a distant relative or a favorite pet dies.

We can help children understand that even though life can never be exactly the same, it will go on. We can let them know that we don't expect them to pick up where they left off before the death. And we can hold out the possibility that at some point their day-to-day life will begin to feel "normal" again. To do that, however, we have to be willing to show children by example what they have to do.

If we have locked ourselves away in our own grief, or given up friends and favorite hobbies, how can our children ever think it's OK to move on with their lives? Parents can send a powerful message that life goes on, that the last thing their deceased loved one would want is for their family to sit at home crying every day.

Peggy Bohme says that learning to adjust is especially difficult because our society doesn't respect people who are grieving. "Death is really considered defeat in our society. People who have not gone through this do not have any idea what is needed until it comes to their own door. It's so overwhelming. Your family is gone; it's a new family. It's a one-parent family, or a one-child family, or a childless family. All of that changes dramatically overnight, and you're expected to forget it."

I can remember cleaning out my mother's dresser after her death and not being able to part with a certain sweater or a favorite dress. Slowly, over the months that followed, I learned to give up those things. Now I have a few select items that remind me of my mother: a birthday letter she left on my pillow years before she became ill, her treasured mother ring, an old cassette tape with a poor-quality recording of her singing. Although the letter is tattered and the ring is misshapen, these things have a physical connection to my mother, and for that reason they are special to me.

It's impossible—and unhealthy—to forget a deceased loved one or friend. In addition to the physical reminders, such as the empty chair at the dinner table or the roadside cross marking where a friend died in a car wreck, people are likely to say things that will make us cringe or cry. ("At least you still have a son," someone told a woman I spoke with who recently lost a daughter to cancer.) Others will tell us how to deal with our grieving children in less-than-helpful ways. ("Just buy him an identical puppy. He'll never know the difference.") Amid all this, we expect children to adjust, even when the adults around them aren't having such an easy time.

In her book *How to Go On Living When Someone You Love Dies*, grief expert Therese Rando explains that after a person dies it takes a while for us to understand completely all the roles he or she played in our lives. Learning to "be in the world" without our loved one reshapes the way we live.

"Readjustment to the new world without your loved one takes great patience and much practice," she says. "It is achieved painfully, step-by-step, as you gradually come to grips with that person not being in your life as he was before." We can remember those words as we work through the grieving process and wait expectantly for our children to do the same. They, too, will be struggling to fill the holes left by their loved one's absence while at the same time keeping that loved one's memory alive in their hearts.

Where and how do we begin?

Talking about a deceased loved one is a good place to start the adjustment process. It may bring back sad memories, but it's a necessary step for everyone's sake. Next, we can create ways to commemorate the life of a deceased loved one, whether through formal events or homemade memorials. If you are an adult helper, you can recommend these activities to families that are dealing with grief and loss, or adapt them for use in your school, classroom, parish, or day care center. Children may want to do one or more of the following:

- Look through photo albums and share memories of their loved one.
- Visit their loved one's favorite restaurant, park, or museum on a birthday or anniversary.

- Plant a tree or flower in memory of their loved one or create a special marker.
- Make a Christmas ornament that will hang on the tree each year in their loved one's memory.
- Visit the cemetery on special occasions.
- Go through their toys and choose some to donate to a charitable organization in their loved one's name.
- Draw pictures or write stories about the times they shared with their loved one. And, if they like, talk about their creations.
- When the time comes, help with the process of cleaning out a loved one's house or giving away a loved one's mementos.
- Volunteer with, or donate a small gift to, their loved one's favorite charity.
- Light a candle at church or at home and say a special prayer for their loved one.
- Create a memory book filled with photos and stories of their loved one.

A remembrance can be anything we want it to be, but it should always include the children. They may even come up with memorial ideas of their own. Children should be allowed to explore and express their feelings. No loss is too small or insignificant to commemorate.

When our German shepherd, Chester, died years ago, we took his leather collar—complete with identification and rabies tags—and buckled it to the handle of my son's little red wagon. Throughout Noah's childhood, every time we visited the park, it was as though Chester was with us. We also bought a small, bone-shaped dog tag and had Chester's name, birth year, and death year etched into it. We tied a red ribbon through it, and each year we hang it on the Christmas tree. Finally, we buried Chester's ashes, along with his first rabies tag and a few dog biscuits, under the big oak tree in our front yard. We put a statue of St. Francis of Assisi on top as a marker. My son knew Chester was buried there and considered it a favorite play spot for piling rocks and raking dirt when he was small. It was our way of letting him know that even though we had a new dog, Greta, to love, we would never forget the one who came before. And it showed him that every life—even a dog's—is worth remembering and celebrating.

Years later, when Greta died, we added her collar to the old wagon handle. The wagon is used for gardening tasks and hauling wood, now that our children have outgrown it, but the collars remain as a concrete reminder of the furry family members we will never forget.

Obstacles to healthy adjustment

No matter how hard we try to prevent or avoid them, inevitable roadblocks will get in the way of a child's adjustment to her new life. We can't remove the people who will make insensitive comments. We can't fill the void left by a loved one's physical absence. We can't make a child move through grief more quickly in order to get to a healthy, well-adjusted place. What we can do is be especially aware of circumstances that may add to a child's grief.

Financial Worries. Often a death in the immediate family can spell financial disaster for the survivors. Funeral costs, loss of salary, insurance issues, mortgages, and other expenses may suddenly become a burden. If a father dies in a car crash, for example, questions about finances that were never really a concern before may now become evident to children. Their mother may need to work outside the home for the first time, or take on a second job. The family may have to move to a smaller house. The children may have to go to day care for the first time. For a child who is trying to accept the loss of a parent, confronting those additional worries makes this adjustment period more difficult.

It can be hard for a surviving parent to keep financial worries quiet, but it's important to try. Children will overhear or pick up on some things regardless of how quiet you try to be. If at all possible, major worries should not be piled on their shoulders. For a parent trying to manage grief, children, and financial worries all at once and all alone, finding support in the form of a sympathetic friend, counselor, or bereavement group can provide a safe place to vent and perhaps brainstorm about solutions without burdening children.

If you are an adult helper and know that a grieving family is struggling financially, offer to be that sympathetic listener, even if you can do nothing else to ease the strain. If a family is in need of emergency assistance to survive financially in the short term, you may be able to put them in contact with assistance organizations. For example, if a surviving parent is cutting expenses, she may no longer be able to afford to keep her child in Catholic school. Many schools will work with parents in that situation to help them maintain a child's school environment until the family is back on its feet financially. Also, keep an eye out for signs that the financial strain is starting to trickle down to the children. Do they seem hungry all the time? Are they late to school more often, perhaps because the car needs repairs or a parent has increased work hours? Children will often provide clues to what's going on, unseen, back at home.

Donna Schuurman of the Dougy Center has seen that responses to such circumstances will vary depending on an individual family's financial situation and the ways people deal with stress. Some families may, in fact, be better off financially after the death of a parent and spouse because of life insurance. Others may be pushed to the brink of bankruptcy or worse. Although children cannot help but be caught up in some of the stress caused by financial issues, they cannot be so involved that their grief is overshadowed by their worry.

"It's a tricky role, not to overburden children and not to make them into premature adults, but also not to withhold information that they already sense," she states. "You don't want to think of everything in catastrophic terms, but for some people, some things are going to have to change. Kids feel that their childhood is being taken away from them."

Role Confusion. When a child loses a sibling or a parent, the family order is disrupted. Perhaps the oldest child is gone, throwing a younger child into the position of eldest for the first time. Or, in an even more dramatic family shift, a surviving sibling is now an only child. Or, a parent dies, and a child is expected to fill the void in either practical or emotional ways.

Without even realizing it, parents and other adults can add to a child's trauma by expecting her to take on a new role that may not be appropriate. It's not uncommon for a girl to hear that she will have to "take care of the family" now that her mother is gone. Boys will inevitably hear that they must be the "man of the house" when their father dies. No child should be expected to take on such an enormous role, especially that of a parent. Attempting to do so while struggling to adjust to life without a loved one will only make this grief task more difficult.

Sonora Thomas's sister Eliza was brutally murdered in Austin, Texas, in 1991. She saw that her own grief was hampered by the fact that she spent most of her time worrying about her grieving parents instead of trying to heal herself.

"I always tried to make my parents happy," she says. "For a long time I felt more sorry for them than I did for myself. I tried everything I could to make the painful feelings go away." When she finally realized she wasn't responsible for her parents' happiness or grief, she was able to move on to her own grief needs.

New Stresses. Keep in mind that this is not the time to institute any other dramatic changes in a child's life—if there is any way to avoid it.

Moving to a new home or town immediately after the death of a parent, for instance, could prove to be beyond traumatic. Suddenly the child is ripped away from the places that hold all the memories of the deceased loved one. The routines, sights, and sounds of life before Dad died are all wrong not only because he is missing but also because the child has been removed from the scene of the relationship.

Changing schools, talking about divorce, even a parent taking on a new job can compound the effects of grief on a child. This is a time when security and stability are needed more than ever.

Donna Schuurman observes that routine provides kids with a sense of comfort. "If a child has to move, he loses his school, his current friends, his home. It has a multiple impact. We encourage people to establish consistency and routines, because even things like dinnertime are usually completely changed if there is a death in the immediate family."

Fueling Fantasies. As parents, we may find ourselves creating stories we think will help children deal with their loss. We pretend Grandpa went on a long trip. We say our dog was sent to live at a farm with lots of room to roam. We stop talking about our deceased spouse or, even worse, forbid our children from talking about their deceased parent.

It may start out as a well-meaning attempt to protect children from too much pain too soon, but before long these actions backfire and we find ourselves with bigger problems. Miriam Klotz, a social worker with Hospice Austin in Texas, offers some advice. One way to help children come to terms with a loved one's absence, she says, is to make sure we don't turn the person's name, memory, favorite foods, and activities into taboo subjects. This behavior creates an unhealthy atmosphere that encourages children to live in a private fantasy world. "This is crucial," Klotz adds, "because otherwise what you're saying is that this part of your life is no longer allowed."

It comes back to the truth. If we withhold it, children will create stories to fill in the blanks, the way I did when I was five years old and didn't get any explanation of my grandfather's death. We're better off taking a deep breath, sitting down with our children, and saying all the things we don't want them to hear from someone else.

Grief has no set timetable

Adjusting to life without a loved one is something children need to be allowed to do at their own pace. It may be months before a child is ready to return to the athletic field knowing that her dad will not be there to cheer for her. Maybe she will never play a particular sport again. That's OK, as long as she knows that it's not a betrayal of her father to go out and kick the soccer ball.

Carol Hyrcza, whose three-year-old son, Peter, drowned during a family outing, remembers how difficult it was for her son Andrew to adjust to life without his brother and best friend. Peter and Andrew had been inseparable. However, on the day of the accident Andrew went out in a boat with the older children while Peter stayed on the shore with his father. It's not surprising, then, that Andrew felt guilty because he did not stay with his brother. As his grief progressed, he had a hard time getting past that guilt.

"When there were other kids around, and he should have been having a fun time, Andrew would get really quiet. I would tell him, 'I know you're thinking of Peter, and he's here now. He'll always be with you.' We talked a lot. Every day we talked about Peter's death. Andrew would say, 'I wonder what he is doing now?' I had him draw pictures. We would go to the cemetery. I would write in a journal, and he would draw pictures of him and Rock (Peter) playing. I would write what they were doing because there was always a story behind the pictures. Now that he is older, he still writes in a journal because he doesn't want to forget any more than I do about those times we had with Peter."

There really isn't any way a child can forget such losses, nor would we want him to. Remembering our deceased loved ones brings them closer for a moment. We hear a favorite song, and for a few brief minutes we imagine that person singing and smiling. We smell apple pie baking in the oven and are taken back to days we will always cherish. Children need to have those memories as well, but they also need to learn that they cannot live in those memories forever.

Parents and other involved adults can watch for behaviors that might signal a need for intervention: a preschooler talks to his deceased father every day as if he is still alive; an elementary-age child continues filling the dog's food dish every day months after he's gone; a preadolescent starts taking on personality traits of her deceased sibling; a teen becomes obsessed with death and violence.

Balance is key in these situations. All the behaviors just mentioned may happen at one time or another as part of the normal grieving process. But when they begin to take on increasing significance in a child's life or start to alter his ability to cope with reality, help is needed. If we know how to read our children, we can intervene before behavior gets out of hand.

Think about how long it takes us adults to adjust to new situations. How many months must pass before we feel comfortable in a new job? How long before we finally get around to calling a new city "home"? How much harder is it, then, for a child to get used to going to bed every night without a kiss and a prayer from Mom? It takes time—and in some ways, it takes forever. It takes a willingness to travel through sadness to a place of acceptance. And, as you will read in the next chapter, it takes a mountain of trust for a child to open his heart and begin to love and live again.

Activity: Creating a Memory Book

Help your child create a scrapbook in honor of your loved one. Use materials and remembrances from around the house to make a simple book your child will treasure. (See alternate Memory Makers in Appendix B.)

Step 1. For the cover, cut a piece of poster board or heavy construction paper into two nine-by-twelve-inch rectangles. (Or you can use a cereal box or cardboard and cover the pieces with wallpaper, fabric, or construction paper.)

Step 2. Allow your child to decorate the cover—provide photos, markers, paints, crayons, glue, glitter, ribbon.

Step 3. Let your child pick out some photos of your deceased loved one to include in the book. If there are other keepsakes you are willing to pass along, provide those as well (pressed flowers, programs from special events, favorite recipes, favorite poems, a birthday or Christmas card, etc.). An older child may want more specific items, such as the obituary from the newspaper or the prayer card from the funeral home.

Step 4. Help your child piece together her favorite memories of your loved one. The child can write down these stories or, if she is too young, dictate the stories to you. Put these down on paper, leaving room for photos and other mementos.

Step 5. Create a "Remember when . . ." page. Ask your child to list some special times she spent with your loved one. (Inside pages can be plain white paper, construction paper, or lined loose-leaf paper—whichever your child prefers.)

Step 6. Leave one page for "Favorites," and list your loved one's favorite food, color, song, poem, book, vacation spot, etc.

Step 7. Allow your child to draw pictures on the pages, maybe even creating a portrait of your loved one to include as an entire page in the book.

Step 8. Collect all of the pages and use a hole punch to put a set of two holes along the left edges of the covers and pages.

Step 9. Group the pages together in whatever order your child prefers and use a ribbon or string to tie the pages and covers together.

Questions for Reflection

» How has day-to-day life for your children changed because of their loss?

» Have they been asked to take on new responsibilities, or have they been burdened with adult tasks and/or roles (physical, emotional, mental) before they are ready?

» Do you find yourself wanting to rush children through grief, or, conversely, pressuring them to ignore their feelings as a way to protect them?

» What are some simple ways you can help your children remember their loved one? Plan one activity or remembrance project to give children the space and direction they need to create a memorial for their loved one.

Meditation: Empty Spaces, Full Hearts

Death thrusts us headlong
into a new reality,
one where the void
left by our loved one
reminds us again and again
of what's missing, who's missing.
Help us show our children by example
how to fill that emptiness
with memories that celebrate
the times we have shared
rather than harbor regrets
over what will never be.

5

Learning to Start Over

- Giving children permission to live again
- Helping children feel safe
- Setting examples of healthy behavior
- When can we expect the grieving to end?
- Moving forward: a practical guide for parents

*Tears of sorrow often pave the way for tears of joy. I will
never take a relationship for granted again, the way I took
for granted my relationship with my sister. For the rest of
my life, I will try to squeeze every last bit of juice out of
love. Losing a love that mattered to me taught me to love
in a way I never would have known.*

—Marianne Williamson, *Everyday Grace*

In the days immediately following my mother's death, there was a
steady stream of visitors to our home. Many of them came bearing
casseroles and cakes, trays of cold cuts, and pots of soup. It was as
though they could keep the grief at bay by feeding us around the clock,
and it was probably one of the most important things anyone did for
us at that point in time. It relieved us of having to think about cooking
or shopping or eating. We sat down and, almost as if by magic, plates
of food appeared before us.

Then our friends and neighbors went back to their old lives. But
this was something they couldn't do for us. We couldn't even do it for
ourselves. We could never go back to what was, only forward to a new
place. When the food stopped arriving and the flowers started wilting,
we were suddenly roused from our grief to find that we were expected
to go on—somehow.

It's a harsh awakening when you realize that the earth does not stop
spinning on its axis just because someone you love has died. People
go about their business. Life, for the most part, goes on without missing a beat. You find yourself asking, *How can this be? Why isn't everyone weeping? Didn't this life mean something?* In the midst of that shock
and disbelief, it is almost impossible to conceive of going on with your
own life.

But when the initial days of official mourning are over, families face
that overwhelming reality. Adults go back to work. Children return to

school. Eventually, everyone in the family is expected to recreate some version of his or her former life. Society gives the bereaved only a few days to "get over" their grief, but it takes much longer than that to plod through the fields of sorrow to a place where the soil is fertile enough to support a new beginning. That's what this fourth grief task is all about: finding a way to move on without forgetting the loved one who is gone.

Children may have an especially difficult time learning to live, laugh, and trust in spite of their grief. They may think that, in going on with their lives, they leave behind their loved one. Perhaps they feel that their ability to go on is somehow disloyal or cruel to the person who is gone. Worse yet, other people may make them feel that way. It is the job of parents and other adults to help children understand that it is normal and healthy to go on living—and even enjoying life—after the death of a loved one.

We can teach children that losing one person does not mean that everyone we love will die. We can show them that it's OK to invest our hearts in new relationships. We can help them find the trust they lost—trust that those around them won't disappear, trust that God is not out to get them, trust that the world is not inherently bad.

According to Donna Schuurman, kids wonder how they can possibly feel good when someone they love is dead. "It's a catch-22. They want to feel better, but you can feel guilty about feeling better. It's a long-term process. Often that's happening at a time when kids are developing in other ways—their bodies are growing, their hormones are changing. It's just a huge additional piece to have to try to figure out, and often they're trying to figure it out alone."

When my grandmother Helen was nearing her 100th birthday and was admitted to the hospital for dehydration, my daughter Chiara, eight years old at the time, said, "I hope she doesn't die." It was one of those teachable moments, and I knew it was time to talk about life and death and my grandmother. I explained that although E-ma might not die that day, she would die soon. And even though we'll be sad when that day comes and we'll miss her, we'll know that she had a good life, and it will be OK.

Chiara looked at me with silent questions flashing in her big brown eyes: *How could it possibly be OK if E-ma dies?* I have to admit that the thought of my grandmother dying brought tears to my eyes even as I told my daughter that all would be well. Yet I needed to help Chiara understand that while we mourn the death of someone we love, we celebrate their life in the midst of it.

When my grandmother eventually took a turn for the worse and died about one year later, Chiara was prepared for it. She had visited E-ma in the nursing home only a few weeks before and had seen her rapid decline. She had seen me crying over what I knew was coming soon. But she also understood that, when losing someone who was almost 101 years old, there was reason to be sad but not reason to be despondent. At the wake, Chiara knelt next to the casket and prayed. At the funeral, she carried the Bible into the church ahead of the casket. She laid a flower on E-ma's grave, and then at a local restaurant just a short while later she raised her glass of soda as we toasted my grandmother's life with both tears and laughter.

Chiara was fortunate in that her first experience with death was "easy" in terms of understanding the how and why of it. The passing of a great-grandmother may be sad, but it's not tragic or incomprehensible or confusing. And we lived two hours away from E-ma and saw her only every few months, so the loss did not impact Chiara's day-to-day life. For many children, their first experience with death and loss is often fraught with questions that have no easy answers and with sorrows that linger for months, even years.

Giving children permission to live again

The death of a loved one can burn a permanent change onto a child's very soul. Learning to live again seems like an impossible request. A teenage boy loses his mother to cancer, and now he is supposed to rent a tux for the prom or put on his football uniform for the big game. It may never happen—the wound may be too fresh or too deep to allow him to reach that point so quickly. By contrast, some children may find comfort in doing "normal" things. That is why it is so important not to judge a child's behavior as a sign of his or her concern, or lack of concern, for the deceased person.

Jennifer Morgan, who talked earlier about her brother's drowning at age fourteen, remembers that the demands of day-to-day life were still there after Robby's death. In a way, these demands forced life to go on. "My parents had three other children to provide for. Julie and I still had to go to softball, piano, and ballet. Peter needed to attend soccer practice and karate."

Jennifer's story isn't uncommon. Life does go on. Adults and children in grief soon learn that going back to ballet lessons, school, work, or ceramics class is healthier than sitting home alone and crying. The question is, how can we help children get from a place of grief to a place where they feel safe enough to rebuild around their loss?

Schuurman says that the process begins by simply allowing children to express their feelings. "This is a continually negotiated process. There is not a magical ending point. Ultimately, forcing children to do things or not allowing them to do things doesn't work too well. It goes back to providing the proper environment, the same way you would for a physical wound, because this is an emotional wound. What you do to allow healing will vary depending upon the severity of the wound, from day to day and person to person."

During this healing period of the grief process, a child may feel a different kind of guilt because she is beginning to enjoy life again and is not always focused on the person who has died. Parents and other adults may expect fears and other symptoms of grief to begin to fade, when in reality such symptoms remain a very big part of the child's healthy grieving.

For Jennifer Morgan, grief was like a roller coaster ride. "You refuse to accept that this has happened. You feel depressed, sad, lonely, like it can't get any worse. Then you begin to laugh again and experience feelings of guilt. Why should I be happy if Robby is dead? I'm still grieving, but life continues. I am very happy. I know I have a special guardian angel who looks out for me. I know I will see him again."

So children may find themselves laughing and happy despite their best efforts to maintain a solemn appearance in memory of the dead friend or family member. And just as quickly they are tossed back into depression over the idea that they could be so cruel as to be happy when a person they love is gone. Guilt takes over and pushes a child's progress back a few steps. Grief doesn't always move forward in a direct and clear path.

As we parents and other caring adults sit on the sidelines and wince for the children in our lives every time they beat themselves up over something that's not their fault, we have to remember that all of this is normal. Kids wouldn't be kids, wouldn't be human, if they didn't feel the same guilt and glee that all of us feel at one time or another. As adults our job is to let them know that it's OK to be happy, that learning to laugh again does not mean we have stopped loving our loved one who is gone now.

Helping children feel safe

There are no magic potions or secret strategies when it comes to helping children adjust to loss or feel safe enough to trust again. Giving them a healthy balance of support and private time is the best approach. From a parent's perspective, however, it can be pretty hard to decide which is needed most when a child is hurting. Our natural instinct makes us want to hug them, hold them tight, and tell them everything will be OK.

Even during minor upheavals in my children's lives, I often don't know whether to hover around trying to engage them or to disappear and let them have time alone. It comes back to reading our children. When my son, Noah, was young, he would put on a tough-guy, no-tears facade, pretending he wasn't hurt or afraid. He would quietly wait for us to recognize his fears and gently ease into the subject, not through direct questioning but through play and art and casual conversations. Our youngest daughter, Chiara, is incredibly sensitive and empathetic, crying over the death of someone she hears about on the news or at church. She wears her fear and sorrow on her sleeve, so it's easy to know when she needs comfort, even if it isn't always easy to know exactly what to say. Our middle daughter, Olivia, appears to roll with the punches from the outside but is quietly processing her grief until it slips out in a casual comment.

Every child is different, and parents and other caregivers often know how a particular child will respond to different approaches. Does he like to be questioned directly about events? Does she prefer quiet closeness, curled up on your lap with a book? Does he want to retreat to his room one minute and then lash out at you the next for not noticing how much pain he is in? Before we get our backs up or let our tempers flare over what seems to be inconsistent or outright hostile behavior, we can reflect on the ways children deal with everyday issues. Then, using that knowledge, we can begin to use familiar parenting and teaching strategies to help children express the things that are bottled up and waiting to come out.

There is one thing of which we can be sure: Children want a safe place to retreat to during the grieving process and a safe place to emerge from when the time comes to move on. We can provide that secure and comfortable haven by making our home, classroom, day care center, sports club, or parish a place where no comments or questions are judged harshly or laughed at or ignored. We can encourage healthy conversations by listening, being truthful and consistent, and fostering an atmosphere in which a loved one's memory becomes a healthy and happy part of a child's life.

It is possible to remember a deceased family member or friend without becoming morbid. Sharing stories, remembering favorite places or events, hanging up a few special photographs—all of these simple actions go a long way toward helping kids keep the memory of a loved one alive.

Grief expert Alan Wolfelt sums it up best in his video *A Teen's View of Grief:* "Normalize but do not minimize." If we can remember those words, we can help children (and parents) find a healthy place to plant the seeds of new life.

Setting examples of healthy behavior

Once children have accepted the reality of a loved one's death and have begun the long process of making that reality part of their lives, how do we help them resume the interests and relationships they had before, and perhaps even forge new ones?

This difficult road will be made smoother if children witness good examples of healthy grief in their parents and other adults who factor prominently in their lives. We can model for children what to do when they experience a loss. As parents, we can allow them to watch us return to our exercise class or book discussion group. We can invite friends over for dinner. We can begin laughing again. We can show children that life goes on. It is changed, for sure, but it can be happy once again. Adults who are outside the family can foster and encourage opportunities for children to experience joy and lightness as we sense they are moving out of the stages of early and deep grief.

However, it's important for us to understand that, even with our best efforts, children who experience the death of a loved one, especially if it is a particularly significant death, will continually renegotiate the issues surrounding that loss. They must do this especially during adolescence, as they enter into new relationships, and as they reach important milestones. For some, these negotiations and adjustments will last into adulthood.

Miriam Klotz, a social worker with Hospice Austin in Texas, says that a child's ability to negotiate successfully depends on whether he has worked through his grief. "Even if a child lost a parent at age five, when he gets to high school graduation his grief will be recognized at that moment. When he gets married, it will again be recognized. At each developmental stage it will come up. With each kind of cognitive development, children will reprocess the whole thing, given the opportunity, and come to different terms with it."

After close to thirty years without my mother, I am at a place now where I am very aware how grief is a shape-shifter, morphing into new forms or showing up unexpectedly all these years later. I'm never surprised by it anymore. I watch it from a distance, observing how easy it is for our heart and mind to experience that woundedness long after we thought the scars had faded. Just this week I was driving home from a doctor's appointment when "The Wind beneath My Wings" came on the radio. That song has always reminded me of my mother. In fact, I had it played at my wedding in her honor as I danced with my father. And there, at a stoplight in the middle of town almost three decades after my mother's death, silent tears rolled down my cheeks as I carried on with my errands. I recognize my grief today. I own it and in some ways enjoy the way it brings back so vividly the memory of my mother.

All children will go through these kinds of regrieving episodes throughout their lives. It is normal and healthy. We can be available to them any time a major milestone or event is on the horizon, or any time children are experiencing extraordinary burdens or joys. We can let them know it's nothing to be ashamed of and nothing to fear. We can help them let the feelings in, reflect on what's happening, and find the good that comes from remembering.

When can we expect the grieving to end?

Children cannot move forward if their daily lives are still heavily inter-twined with thoughts of a deceased relative or friend. They must come to a clear understanding that they can hold onto the memories of that person and, at the same time, move ahead with the next phase of their lives, whatever and whomever that may include. They do have to take those memories and find an appropriate place for them.

It is unlikely that children will ever feel that the issue of loss is com-pletely resolved, especially if the person who died played a pivotal role in their lives. It is key that parents and other adults create an atmos-phere in which healing can take place, allowing children to talk about the deceased loved one if that is what they want, but not forcing them to talk if they prefer to be silent. Providing opportunities for rituals around anniversaries, holidays, and birthdays is also an important part of the process at this stage.

Jennifer Morgan says that the first Christmas after Robby's death was very difficult. There was no Christmas tree. Their family dinner, which was normally hosted at her house, was moved to an aunt's house instead. "It was really awful. I remember being ten, sitting in my aunt's house, all the gifts a kid could want, but feeling this numbness. All the forced smiles were hiding sad faces. Christmas was our favorite time of year, and I wondered if it would ever be the same."

The answer to that, of course, is no, it will never be the same. But eventually it can be happy. Although the first anniversary, birthday, and major holidays after a loved one's death are usually painful and sad, it is important to find ways to commemorate those occasions in positive ways. What was Dad's favorite food? Go to a restaurant and order it. What was Mom's favorite activity? Pile the kids in the car and do it. Getting outside, sharing happy memories, and doing something fun are healthy ways to show kids that they can remember the person who is gone with laughter as well as with tears.

Pediatrician Alan Greene notes that people get into the most trouble during the holidays if they force themselves to be happy and refuse to acknowledge who is missing or how the special day has changed. "Take a few minutes right at the beginning of the celebration to say, 'This is really hard. Last year we had Mom with us. This year we don't, and it is really hard.' Acknowledge that at the very beginning. Everybody will feel sad, but then the rest of the holiday can be really uplifting," he says. "If it floats around as this big something missing the entire time, then the holidays become nothing but a drain."

Carol Hyrcza and her family have found unique ways of commemorating her son Peter's life on days that hold special meaning for them. "On June 29, the day Peter died, we go to the cemetery with donuts and chocolate milk, and we sit there and eat. Then we do something fun together," she says. "On his birthday, we have people over, watch a video of him, and have dinner. On Halloween, he gets a pumpkin. This Christmas we brought a Christmas tree to the cemetery."

We can't be afraid to mention our deceased loved one's name or talk about the times we shared. Look through photos, play Grandma's favorite song, bake Mom's special cookie recipe, visit the park Grandpa used to love. If we are adult caregivers or teachers, we can encourage children in our care to talk about their loved one if we sense they are stuck in a bad place. Also, we can give them opportunities to create something in their loved one's memory. Perhaps a pinecone birdfeeder for the backyard, a Christmas wreath to hang on their bedroom door, or a poem they can tuck into their nightstand and pull out whenever they feel sad. Kids will relish the opportunity to remember the loved one who is missing. Better yet, they will learn that remembering and commemorating are not signs of weakness but signs of strength and growth.

Moving forward: a practical guide for parents

Let your children see that you are engaging in your favorite hobbies, friendships, and interests. Not only will it help them understand that it's OK for their lives and their happiness to flourish, but it also will help you regain some sense of normalcy for yourself.

Encourage—but don't force—your children to resume sports, music, or art. You need to give your children permission to return to the things they love, even if it is without the person they love. They need to know that you will not be angry with or disappointed in them if they want to go back to Little League or ballet class. On the other hand, avoid the urge to pressure children into something they're not ready to do. If you encourage a child to return to a much-loved activity and he balks at the notion, back off. He will let you know when he is ready.

Provide a safe, secure, and stable environment at home. Keep mealtimes the same, and try to eat at least one meal a day together as a family. Be available to your child as much as possible, and continue to keep the same rules around the house. Children need the routine of chores, curfews, family dinners, and nightly walks. Whatever it is that made your family run well before your loss can help get things back on track after your loss.

Avoid adding new stresses until your children have adjusted to their loss. It may be financially necessary for a parent to take on a new job after a death in the family. However, if at all possible, parents should avoid making drastic changes in their own lives and the lives of their children. Kids who are coping with the loss of someone close to them will be hard-pressed to make additional adaptations. New jobs that take parents away or require changes in childcare are especially troublesome. The same holds true for moves to new towns or new school districts. Now is the time to keep things as steady and familiar as possible.

Activity: Marking an Anniversary

The anniversary of a loved one's death can be an especially difficult time, but it doesn't have to be all sorrow and mourning. You can honor your loved one in a way that celebrates his life and lifts your spirit.

Have a special family dinner and serve your loved one's favorite foods. It doesn't matter if they don't necessarily go together—be creative. If your loved one liked pancakes, pasta, and apple pie, then that can be the menu. Don't get stuck on the idea of a formal or fancy affair—unless, of course, that's what your loved one liked. The dinner can reflect your loved one's personality.

- **At the dinner table**, have each person share a favorite memory of your loved one or say a special prayer.
- **After dinner** (or before) go to a park, museum, or other spot that was a favorite of your loved one, or do something she loved to do—walk in the woods, play miniature golf, go out for ice cream.
- If you're not up to planning a dinner, go out to your loved one's favorite restaurant—maybe order her favorite meal in her honor.

If a special dinner isn't optimal, there are plenty of other ways to mark a loved one's anniversary or birthday:

- **Go to Mass together** as a family early in the morning and then go out to breakfast or to the cemetery, or both.
- **Release a balloon** in your loved one's memory and watch it disappear into the clouds.
- **Get a bottle of bubbles** and blow your sorrows into the wind.
- **Go to your loved one's grave** and leave a special stone or some other small token of your affection.
- **Gather friends and family** and watch videos of your loved one and look through photo albums. Share stories and remember the happy times you had together.

Questions for Reflection

» Is your child refusing to resume normal activities? If so, is there one small way to introduce a favorite hobby or pastime and invite your child to respond?

» Try to assess the atmosphere around your child, whether at home or in the classroom or in the day care center. Is it an atmosphere that encourages questions and discussions without judgment? Do children feel free to express their fears, anger, confusion, sadness? What can you do to make the atmosphere more supportive?

» If you are in grief as well, are you modeling healthy behavior? Are there things you could do today to take a step in the right direction?

» Are there any anniversaries, birthdays, or holidays coming up that might be especially difficult for your child? If so, look for ways to make the day special and celebrate your loved one's life.

» Are you giving your child the space and permission to lead the way through his grief, even if it takes longer than you expect it should?

Conversely, if your child is stuck in a particularly dark place for an extended period of time, can you find an outside support group to help?

Meditation: Milestones

They say time heals all wounds,
but it does not erase the scars.
We may recover,
but we never forget,
and that is a blessing in disguise.
Day after day, year after year
we carry our loved ones with us,
in our hearts, in our memories,
celebrating their lives
until we meet again.

6

When the Unthinkable Happens

- School shootings, near and far
- Talking about suicide
- Homicide, fires, and other violent deaths
- Handling the death of a child
- Miscarriage, stillbirth, and infant death
- Social media and its role in modern grief
- Dealing with difficult circumstances

*Going home was difficult. How do you tell your children
that their baby sister is going to die? I do not recall the
words we used, or even what the children said in reply. But
I will never forget the sound of their weeping, the sight of
my sons holding each other in comfort, my daughters
huddled together, their shoulders shaking, eyes swollen.*
—Catherine Adamkiewicz, *Broken and Blessed:
A Life Story*

Too often in recent times we have watched the frightening images on television as children are led—or carried on stretchers—away from their schools. Newtown, Littleton, Springfield, Jonesboro, Paducah, Conyers, Pearl, Edinboro—these towns are known to us for only one reason. And those places are just the biggest and most deadly shootings. This sort of violence has become so commonplace in our world that the loss of "just" one or two lives doesn't even warrant a permanent place in our memory banks. But for those whose lives are touched directly by such violence, every life, every moment, every "what if" will be etched onto their hearts for all time. For children, such losses may profoundly change their lives and leave permanent marks.

Some children are right there, hiding in a closet, trying not to breathe too loud lest they be discovered. Others may be wounded or forced to run for their lives. And others watch from a distance on television, fearing deep down that it could just as easily have been their schools, their friends, their lives. The now-normal routine of school lockdown drills reinforce the fears, as children of all ages cower in classrooms and cafeterias and closets in an attempt to "practice" for possible realities that no one can understand or predict.

While school shootings have, unfortunately, become the most obvious and glaring examples of tragic and violent deaths in our society, they are by no means the only unthinkable losses forced upon some children. From the monumentally horrific, such as the terrorist attacks of September 11, 2001, to the personally devastating, such as suicide within the immediate family, many children have to grapple with losses that would level most adults. And even if they are not directly involved with the tragedy, often they soak up enough sorrow from the periphery that they become fearful and sad without fully understanding why.

School shootings, near and far

Children affected directly by such tragedies have to deal with a kind of grief most of us cannot imagine. Schools should be places of safety, learning, and fun. How do children ever return to school and move past the pain? How can adults help children understand what we ourselves can't wrap our heads around? It's like a tightrope walk for parents, teachers, grief counselors, and other adults who must somehow alleviate fears that we ourselves can't shake.

Whenever we're dealing with a terribly traumatic situation, such as a school shooting or terrorist attack, whether close to home or far away, first we have to get *our* fears and emotions in check. We can start by turning off the television, as well as disconnecting ourselves from Internet or smartphone news for awhile. Yes, we need to be informed, but we don't need to live and breathe the endless loop of horror that TV and Internet news has become in this country. It will only feed our fears and anxieties, as well as that of our children. And while it may be fairly easy to regulate the viewing habits of young children, teenagers with smartphones raise this issue to a new level. They will often see news as it's happening, perhaps even before parents or other adults are aware. It's important to sit down with teens and talk about what they're reading and hearing, what's being said on social media and texted between friends. For more tips on how to deal with this technological twist on trauma, see the section later in this chapter labeled "Social media and its role in modern grief."

When we try to help children deal with actual violent or traumatic losses—or with fears over reports they've heard about violence—it helps if we let the children lead the way. An article, "Talking with Kids about News: Strategies for Talking and Listening" on the Public Broadcasting System (PBS) website, offers this advice: "Start by finding out what your child knows. When a news topic comes up, ask an open-ended question to find out what she knows like, 'What have you heard about it?' This encourages your child to let you know what she is thinking."

The rest of the strategy includes asking follow-up questions, explaining events using simple and age-appropriate language, listening to and acknowledging a child's feelings, and offering reassurance.

"When a child is exposed to disturbing news, she may worry about her safety. To help her calm down, offer specific examples that relate to her environment like, 'That hurricane happened far away but we've never had a hurricane where we live.' Actions speak louder than words—so show your child how you lock the door if she gets scared by a news report about robbers, point out the gutters and storm drains if a hurricane story causes fear, and explain what the security guards do at the airport after a story about terrorists," the PBS guide notes.

In a related video, Fred Rogers, known affectionately by generations of PBS viewers as Mr. Rogers, offers some advice of his own:

"What children probably need to hear most from us adults is that they can talk with us about anything and that we will do all we can to keep them safe in any scary time."

Mr. Rogers told a story from his own childhood to help parents better understand what might alleviate their children's fears:

My mother would say to me, "Look for the helpers. You will always find people who are helping." To this day, especially in times of "disaster," I remember my mother's words, and I am always comforted by realizing that there are still so many helpers—so many caring people in this world.

At the Ferncliff Presbyterian Camp and Conference Center in Little Rock, Arkansas, ministers and counselors set out to help the children whose lives were touched by the school shooting in nearby Jonesboro back in 1998. What began as a local effort soon developed into an international program to help children affected by violence of all kinds—school shootings, war, or gang activity.

David Gill, a Presbyterian minister and executive director of Ferncliff, says that the children in his program needed to move beyond the deep grief of the initial experience. They had an incredible need to talk, write, and think about what had happened to them.

"We were in uncharted territory," he remembers. "Our philosophy going into this was that the typical church camp experience—being close to nature, forming community, recreation, worship, and reflection—are healing things, so why not take those same components and infuse them into special programs?" The result was a series of camps to help children deal with the aftermath of violence. One camp, Connection 2000, spawned a national effort—TOUCH (Teens Offering Understanding, Caring, Healing)—to connect children who are dealing with this unusual kind of grief and help them on the road to healing.

"The kids said that they wanted to move from being victims to being leaders," cites Gill. "They wanted to help others. They said they didn't want to be treated like broken, fragile people, but instead they wanted to look at how this experience could make them stronger."

In a letter from one of the girls who attended a camp at Ferncliff in 1998, published on the blog of Fourth Presbyterian Church, the power of such programs to help children heal is evident in her words:

My name is Sara. Although we have never met, you supporters of Ferncliff changed my life. On March 24, 1998, there was a shooting at my school similar to the one at Sandy Hook Elementary in Newtown, Connecticut. At the time, I was eleven. I lost my dear friend of four years that day. I can tell you now that if it had not been for the wonderful support we received from Ferncliff in that aftermath, many young lives would have also been lost to the fallout. When you witness such cruelty in the world at such a young age, it is very easy to believe pain and violence are the only things that exist. I thank you from the bottom of my heart for showing our community that love truly is stronger than hate. The memories of those special camps are priceless to me. They help me to see that something positive can come from something so horrific. It also shows me that God has a plan, even if we cannot see it sometimes through the chaos. I will marry my best friend this July, whom I met at a Ferncliff-sponsored lock-in. Thank you for doing God's work. I implore you to continue. Sara.

Talking about suicide

When Amy Biancolli's husband, Chris Ringwald, jumped to his death from the roof of a three-story parking garage near their home, she faced the monumental task of helping their three children come to terms with their father's suicide and work through their grief while also dealing with her own overwhelming sorrow, guilt, anger, and fears.

In her book *Figuring Sh!t Out: Love, Laughter, Suicide, and Survival*, she writes:

> Chris's madness and suicide will never make sense. We will never understand it. My friend Jo calls it a "sorrowful mystery," and I agree—realizing, finally, that I can comprehend his death only as something incomprehensible.
>
> I share this thought with the kids. They absorb it quickly and completely, having witnessed the six-month change in their father and accepted the fact that their "real" dad, their *well* dad, didn't

choose to leave them and this life. Children are deeper than adults, wiser, because they're accustomed to not having all the information. They already know they can't know everything.

Children *are* wise, especially when it comes to grief. Donna Schuurman of the Dougy Center recalled one little boy in a bereavement group for children who had suffered traumatic losses. He wanted the other kids in the group to guess how his dad had died. "The kids were saying, 'He drowned in a pool.' He said, 'Nope.' 'He shot himself in the head?' Again, he said, 'Nope.' They were saying all these macabre things and getting a kick out of it because they couldn't guess. It turned out that he hanged himself. The child illustrated it. He pulled at his neck and fell to the ground. The other children just looked at him. He said, 'He put a rope around his neck and stood on a chair.' They all said, 'Why would he do that?' There was silence, and then the boy, who was four years old, said, 'Because he didn't know how much we loved him.'"

Hearing that story made me want to cry. We don't like to think of children talking about death—especially a parent's death—in those terms. A guessing game? That can't be healthy, right? Yet making a game of it was how this child was able to deal with his sadness, his fears, and his confusion. He was in a grief support group with his peers, children who had experienced similar tragedies. He knew he was safe, so he let down his guard and said what he felt. He knew that his father felt unloved—not that he didn't love his father enough, but that his father didn't comprehend just how much he did love him. That's a pretty healthy understanding for a four-year-old facing loss by suicide.

Not all children will cope so well, and often that's not through any fault of their own. According to Schuurman, the stigma attached to certain kinds of deaths can cause additional stress for children in grief. "Some complications make grief more difficult. It has to do with how society views suicides, or how society views homicides, and how the family has to deal with the dragged-out process: the media, the legal system, the sense of unfairness of things, the closure of a trial. It can go on for years."

When I was doing the research for this book, I traveled around the Internet, stopping in on web pages run by suicide hotlines and prevention organizations as well as much more personal sites put up by family members struggling with the aftermath of a loved one's suicide. Some of them were painfully honest; all of them were heartbreaking. No one wants to talk about suicide—but we have to. It's out there. It's taking our children in increasing numbers. It devastates those who are left behind.

According to the American Foundation for Suicide Prevention, someone in the United States dies by suicide every 12.9 minutes. In 2012, the most recent statistics available, 40,600 suicide deaths were reported in the United States, according to the foundation's website. As if those statistics aren't sobering enough, here are some more. According to the American Academy of Child and Adolescent Psychiatry, suicide is the third leading cause of death for fifteen- to twenty-four-year-olds, and the sixth leading cause of death for five- to fourteen-year-olds. And those numbers are on the rise.

Experts say that death by suicide, homicide, and AIDS are among those most likely to be hidden from children. And yet children almost always know the real reason for a loved one's death. What they don't always understand is why everyone is being so hush-hush about it. It makes them feel as though there is something to be ashamed of. It adds to their guilt, and it can disrupt the healthy grieving that needs to take place.

Grief therapist Linda Goldman, author of *Bart Speaks Out: Breaking the Silence on Suicide*, states on her website that adults need to "explore the topic of suicide openly if we are to break through the barriers of shame and secrecy that accompany this topic and create fertile ground for the resolution of this complicated grief situation."

She affirms that suicide, homicide, AIDS, violence, and abuse create traumatic emotional issues that keep the child from the "normal flow" of grief. "So often a child cannot say that their special person died because they would have to say how that person died," she says. Goldman refers to these unresolved issues as "frozen blocks of time" that create "a wall of ice between the child and his or her grief."

As difficult as the subject is, parents and other adults can find ways to talk honestly about suicide. Children who lose a loved one to suicide are likely to be confused, guilty, embarrassed, or in denial. We can help by telling them, in simple and caring ways, what has happened. Answer questions openly, but consider a child's age and developmental level when deciding how much detail to reveal. Explain that the person who died had an illness of the mind. Don't be judgmental or speak of suicide in terms of morality. Be sure the child knows that the person who died loved him and that he is in no way responsible for what happened. Children affected by suicide are likely to benefit from talking to other survivors, so be sure to contact a suicide support organization for additional assistance (see "Resources for Healing").

Even a suicide that does not affect a child in any direct way can frighten the child and affect daily behavior. When I was writing this book, my daughter Chiara, age nine, became hysterical one night when her father and I told her to go to bed. After trying to ask questions that might help us understand what had caused the outburst, she finally told us through shoulder-shaking sobs that it was because of something one of her friends had told her at a sleepover party five nights earlier. They were watching a movie, and another little girl told her that the star of the movie had killed himself "because he didn't like how his life was going."

Chiara looked at us wide-eyed and asked, "How did he do it?" We skirted around that question and went back to the friend's message. We explained that Robin Williams, the star in question, had a mental illness that made it impossible for him to realize that suicide was not the answer to his problems, that it was terribly sad for the people he left behind, and that suicide is never the answer to any life problem. We talked for a while more. She told us she was both sad and scared by the idea of suicide. Her big sister, Olivia, stayed in her room with her that night, which eased her troubled mind, but I have no doubt we'll come back around to this suicide question at a later date. So be aware of stories your children may be hearing outside the home. You can't always control it, but you can be there to listen, answer questions, and comfort them when they are afraid.

Homicides, fires, and other violent deaths

Sonora Thomas was thirteen when her older sister, Eliza, was brutally murdered along with three other teens in Austin, Texas, in what came to be known as "The Yogurt Shop Murders." She says that it was not until the arrest of her sister's alleged killers eight years later that she began to feel a sense of closure. Seeing the men in a courtroom was a turning point in her grief. "I realized that there are actual people who did this and that this was really part of my life. These [defendants] were only a few years older than me, and they were younger than my sister."

Sonora remembers that people did not know what to say to her after her sister's murder. Most people avoided the subject completely. The one person who helped her was a teacher who knew her sister. He simply came up to her and said how sorry he was and that he couldn't believe what had happened. "I wanted that acknowledgment, anything that would take me to the present," she says. One thing that helped was the comfort of being in church. "I am not Catholic, but I went to the Catholic church near my house many times. I would just sit there and cry and cry and pray and pray. I didn't know where else to go."

Something like a homicide can do more than instill a deep sense of grief. It can also cause fears to well up, especially if the murder occurred at or near the child's home—as it did in Sonora's case. "That place was only five blocks from my house," she says. "I spent hours there. That's my neighborhood. It's so violating. Even now I have a hard time going out at night. I have become hyper-aware of things."

Adults trying to comfort children who have suffered a loss due to homicide or suicide need to keep in mind the additional complications that come along with this kind of grief. There will be more fears, more guilt, and more confusion. It's hard to lose a loved one regardless of the circumstances. When you pile assault or other types of violence on top of that loss, it can drive children deep into themselves or cause them to lash out at those around them.

Talk as honestly as you can about what has happened, but don't allow children to get caught up in gory details and sensational news reports. Be aware that others will be talking as well, maybe even pointing fingers and whispering. All of this will be an incredible burden for children. You don't want to lie or keep basic information from them, but you do want to shield them from unnecessary harm. It's important to strike a delicate balance, although it is likely to be toppled by even minor glitches. Be prepared for extreme behaviors and emotions. In this kind of situation it is wise to contact a grief support group or a counselor who specializes in issues surrounding homicide and other violent or tragic death so that children have a safe place to talk about what they're feeling.

According to *Best Practices of Youth Violence Prevention*, a sourcebook put out by the National Center for Injury Prevention and Control, the homicide rate for young people in the United States is the highest among developing countries. More than 4,800 children between the ages of ten to twenty-four were victims of homicide in 2010 alone. Homicide is the second leading cause of death among fifteen- to twenty-four-year-olds. In the inner cities, where gang violence has become all too common, homicide is the leading cause of death among African American males between the ages of fifteen and twenty-four.

Children directly affected by gang violence and other violent deaths are going to have bouts of grief and mourning that are foreign to many of the adults around them. In such cases, peer support and even peer counseling can offer a kind of outlet for pent-up emotions that parents simply cannot provide.

A key point to remember when dealing with children who are experiencing this kind of grief is that they were not blank slates when the violence occurred. Some may have been stinging from their parents' recent divorce; others may have been abused; still others may be caught in drug addiction. When we start digging down into their grief and their raw emotions, it's hard to know if the volcanoes that erupt are due strictly to the violence they experienced or to the other losses and problems they deal with every day. This is true for any child in grief. Their losses will be compounded by any other losses or problems in their lives.

Even after kids have dealt with the initial shock of their experiences, feelings of grief will come back to them in more muted tones over the months and years that follow. Donna Schuurman says that such grief is part of a lifelong process because any major loss is woven into the fabric of our beings. She pointed to the 1999 massacre at Columbine High School in Littleton, Colorado. "At Columbine, when school started up again, people there talked about how they painted the library and moved it, saying, 'We survived.' If you weren't directly impacted, you may be able to do that a lot easier than somebody whose brother was killed. For those kids, life will never be the same. Everything is different."

This statement is true of just about every major loss children face. Everything is different. The losses will shape them, color them, maybe even change their futures. When the grief becomes less intense and the mourning is over, the death will still be there, residing in the recesses of their hearts and minds. It may change their perceptions of the world, of God, of family, and of themselves. And it will stay with them forever.

For the child who witnesses any violent death of a loved one or friend, the size and scope don't really matter. If a child sees her father die in a gruesome car crash or witnesses her sibling being beaten to death, it will be hard for her to get beyond those vivid images. Nightmares and extreme fears are likely to set in. A child may be afraid to get in a car for fear that she will die in a crash or to let her surviving parent drive a car for similar reasons. If the death was at the hands of someone else, there may be fantasies of revenge.

Witnessing a violent death adds extra weight to the already heavy load that grief piles on the shoulders of our children. This may be a case where no amount of hugging and listening will calm their fears. Professional counseling and ongoing support through a grief organization can help start the healing process.

Handling the death of a child

How do you tell a little girl that she has only a few short weeks to live? How do you answer her questions and calm her fears when you have so many of your own to deal with? Once again, children themselves often provide the comfort and prepare the way for us. They can be wise and courageous—if we let them speak their minds.

Mercy Sister Judith Carron, a chaplain at Cardinal Glennon Children's Hospital in St. Louis, remembers the first child who asked her point-blank if she was going to die. Her name was Andrea, a bright little eight-year-old girl with congestive heart failure. "I turned the question back to her so I could have a better understanding of what she understood. I asked her if she thought she was going to die. She said that she did. I said, 'Andrea, I think you are going to die. We don't know when.' She said she was afraid of being alone. The hospital was noisy, and people kept shutting her door. She didn't like that because it scared her. She was afraid of the dark, and she was afraid of the machines."

Andrea was one of those children who wanted to talk about dying and who was lucky enough to find someone to listen. Her heart was failing, but her spirit was strong. She was seeking reconciliation before her death, and Sister Carron helped her find it.

"She asked me if God was going to be mad at her because she had had a fight with her sister before she went to the hospital," says Sister Carron. "She really wanted to connect with her sister, but they lived a distance away. I suggested that she draw a picture and write a card to her sister because children can express so much through art." Andrea made a card for her sister, telling her how sorry she was for the fight they had. It gave her the peace of mind she needed.

Sister Carron also asked Andrea if there was anything she wanted. Andrea asked for a make-up kit, complete with lipstick and powder. "Andrea was pretty bluish because of her lack of oxygen. I had a sense she was putting on a new face. It was as though she was preparing herself for meeting God," Sister Carron recalls. "She died a very peaceful death. We made sure she wasn't alone, that she wasn't in the dark."

Andrea may seem to be a rare child, not only facing her own death but actually preparing for it. Then again, according to Sister Carron, children are better equipped than we suspect for handling this kind of overwhelming tragedy. Even when children have not been told that they are dying, there are clues that they may understand more than they let on.

One boy told his mother about a recurring dream: He was drowning and trying to come up for air. Every time he tried to come up, he went back under the water. Once the mother got up the courage to ask her son what the dream meant to him, a conversation about death evolved naturally.

"I don't think there is just one way to help a child understand he is dying. It is important to try to assess where the child is, to listen to his questions. You don't just say, 'You're dying,'" says Sister Carron. "Some children will tell you something through art and language and symbols. They don't always tell you directly."

Another little boy who was diagnosed with leukemia drew a picture of a body of water with lots of waves. A helicopter with a big hook hanging from it hovered over the water. Bobbing around in the waves was a little boat with a person in it. Sister Carron asked the boy about the picture. Not surprisingly, he said that he was the person in the boat and that he wanted to be rescued by the helicopter. The picture opened the door to a deeper discussion about his leukemia.

Emma Duke was only twenty-seven months old when she was diagnosed with cancer. She was four years old when she died. During those intervening years, Emma underwent treatment upon treatment and was always told the truth about what was happening to her. Her mom, Kathy, says that through it all Emma held onto the hope that when she was well enough the family would go to Disneyland.

"By the time she got off treatment, she was so weak and so sick. We were trying to build her up, but she relapsed," Kathy says. Despite her condition, Emma continued to hope, saying, "Disneyland soon." But Disneyland never happened for Emma. Her treatments made her weak and even caused her to lose her hearing.

"We didn't realize we were going to lose contact with her in such a profound way. It was really hard to communicate. She was in such bad shape," Kathy says. "At the very end I finally whispered to her, 'You don't have to be miserable. You can go if you need to.' She grabbed my hand and said, 'I love you, Mom.'"

At the same time Emma was confronting her own death, her brother, Joseph, was dealing with the inevitable loss of his sister. The two were very close and Joe adored his little sister. He was with Emma every step of the way and was devastated by her death.

The siblings of children who die from cancer or other long-term illnesses suffer their own kind of special grief, a grief that in some ways starts before the death actually occurs. Often it is grief over a childhood disrupted or lost, grief over the loss of a parent's attention, grief over the loss of an active playmate and partner, or grief over the loss of the life they once knew.

Sister Carron says that parents are often torn between the sick child and the healthy children, and they tend to give more attention to the sick child. "It's important for parents to spend some alone time with the well children, especially with younger children, although teenagers will feel the absence of a parent as well."

Parents can look for support through church and community organizations as well as among family members and friends. The well child may benefit from something as simple as a trip with Mom or Dad to the hospital cafeteria or the nearest McDonald's. Remember, though, that kids in this kind of situation will often be envious of the attention the sick child is getting. That doesn't make them bad kids. It makes them normal.

After the death of a child, siblings may grapple with additional guilt, anger, questions, and fears. Funeral director Peter Assumma says that when he talks to siblings, he first makes sure that they understand how extraordinary the situation is. For most kids, he says, the biggest fear is that they are going to die as well. "We need to be able to take that fear away from that child. We need to help that child recognize that it is so extraordinary for a child to die."

Assumma also has found that parents' typical reaction is to shield their surviving children from the death of a sibling. In his experience, however, as soon as a child is a toddler he is old enough to be included in the events surrounding a brother's or sister's death.

"You want the child to understand that a family deals with everything together—good and bad," he says. "Children should not be prevented from being a part of it and really should play a role if they are old enough to have known their brother or a sister."

Miscarriage, stillbirth, and infant death

When Cathy Adamkewicz lost her daughter, Celeste, her seventh child, to a rare heart condition at four months of age, Cathy was deep in her own grief. Yet somehow she and her husband, Adam, had to step outside their darkness to help their children deal with the death of their baby sister. It helped that throughout Celeste's short life they had tried to "normalize" things by bringing the children to the hospital and talking openly about Celeste's condition. Although they were devastated by her death, they found ways to focus on and celebrate the gifts of Celeste's life.

"I was surprised by how well they handled it. I think it helped that I let them know that whatever feelings they were experiencing—including relief—were acceptable," Cathy recalls, adding that she and her husband "continued to normalize the death experience, even though the death of a child hardly feels normal to anyone."

They encouraged their children to participate in the funeral planning and the funeral Mass, which they did. They were invited to place something in Celeste's casket if they wanted to, and the youth group their teens were involved in provided music for the liturgy. Cathy and

Adam also encouraged their children to spend time with their friends as much as they wanted to during this difficult period.

"Overall I think the fact that our family was extremely close to begin with was highly beneficial. We had been homeschooling at that time for many years, which gave us a unique foundation of togetherness. We could not have fathomed how our efforts at building a strong sense of family identity would serve us in such a profound way," Cathy explains. "The little rituals we had shared—things like reading together—became a great comfort to the children and to me."

For the Adamkewicz family, faith played a critical role. Cathy says that their Catholic faith is so integral to their lives, she can't even imagine going through an experience like Celeste's death without it. Their faith in the resurrection, she says, allowed them to see Celeste's life and death as "beautiful and meaningful events."

"Ten years later, we continue to talk about how God allowed her to be born, to suffer and die, and to do it in the context of our family. We look at it as a grace. And somehow, even as the events were unfolding, we were able to see them in the light of this faith," Cathy adds.

Over the years, Celeste's memory has resurfaced again and again in ways both sorrowful and joyful. Both of Cathy's daughters married in 2007 and mourned the fact that Celeste was not there to be their flower girl. On Celeste's birthday and her "birthday into heaven" the family continues to remember her with cake and celebrations. It's the more ordinary days when grief can sneak up on you and catch you unaware, Cathy says.

She suggests that other parents going through a similar loss simply try to be present to their children. "Listen to them and let them know that anything they are thinking or feeling is OK. Let them know that you are upset too, but that you know that you are all going to be OK. Offer to take them to counseling, and go yourself to show them how normal and acceptable it is to ask for help," she says.

"I would also remind them that the grieving process has no end point. The loss of a child is permanent, but who you become, and what your family becomes, is ever-changing. You and your family will get to a new place. The grief will sometimes emerge so sharply that it will take your breath away, but it will not become the whole of who you are," she added. "I am convinced that with the faith in Our Lord, who holds our loved ones close to his heart as our touchstone, we can become more compassionate, grace-filled versions of our former selves. Have hope. And know that we will be reunited with them some day, and our joy will be eternal, and our tears truly washed away."

The death of an unborn baby may be especially difficult for little ones to understand. Parents go from excited and happy to distraught and sad seemingly overnight. In many cases, the other children are still quite young, making things even more challenging. A child is going to ask questions, either out loud at the dinner table or in the silence of his or her inner world: *What's wrong with Mommy and Daddy? Where did the baby go? Did I do something to make it happen? How can a baby die before she's even born?*

When I lost a baby through miscarriage, my son was only one and a half years old. He was too young to understand what was happening. In fact, he was too young to even know that I was pregnant. He did know that Mommy was crying a lot and that we were running from one doctor's office to another. He was with us when the midwife couldn't find the heartbeat, when the ultrasound technician confirmed what we already suspected, and when we sat in a long line at the hospital arranging the details of what had to be done. He saw my tears and heard my sobbing, but he was still too young to comprehend why.

When I became pregnant again, my husband and I were very careful about what we told Noah. We didn't tell him about the baby until we had heard the heartbeat. Even up until the day Olivia was born we were careful to phrase things in ways that wouldn't harm Noah if something horrible were to happen. Every time we told him not to bang into Mommy's belly or jump on Mommy unexpectedly, we worried that if something happened to our unborn baby he would hold himself responsible. He had, on more than on occasion, expressed concern that he would do something and "the baby would never come out." So children can internalize the things they hear and see.

When it comes to miscarriage, stillbirth, or infant death, we have to talk to our children about the sad reality and stress that nobody is to blame. Children need to hear that they had no part in the tragedy. They need to know that sometimes babies are not healthy enough or strong enough to make it to birth, that sometimes they have problems with their hearts or their lungs or any number of other ailments that cause them to die when they should be staring wide-eyed at a whole new world.

Don't be surprised if very young children become more clingy or fearful after the death of an unborn baby or infant. This is a scary thing for everyone involved, and children will feel the effects of such a loss just as their parents do—perhaps not to the same degree, but there will be pain and sadness. Pretending it didn't happen or trying to act as though it is not a big deal doesn't do anyone any good, least of all the children. Acting as though it is not upsetting to lose a child will only add to the surviving child's insecurities and fears: *Would Mommy and Daddy be upset if something happened to me? Isn't it sad when a baby dies?* Simply speak in terms children can understand, be prepared for hard questions, and be willing to cry together.

Social media and its role in modern grief

When it comes to public tragedies and deaths, we now have a modern dynamic at play in the grieving process: social media. It wasn't that long ago that parents and other adults could shield children from news reports of the scariest, most violent tragedies and give them the story at home in the context of shared family values, faith, and love. Today, however, many children—especially teens—are plugged into social media on a near-constant basis. Stories and photos scroll through their feeds or in comments, and children start to process information in isolation or with only the voices of their equally uninformed or, even worse, misinformed friends echoing in their heads.

This wash of information can leave a child grappling with incredibly difficult news without the benefit of adult guidance, insight, or comfort. By the time they get to us or tell us what they've heard, it may be too late to undo the damage. What's the answer? Experts say the best thing a parent can do is to sit down with your child and explain it on your terms and from your perspective *before* a kid on the bus or in the cafeteria or on Twitter does it for you, only not nearly as well.

"Less sheltering from the truth is one way you can be proactive and give children the messages you want them to hear," says Dianna Masto, a New York-based licensed clinical social worker who specializes in children's therapy.

Masto notes that children have always been able to get information from outside parental circles, but social media now makes it easier and more likely. "It's another way for kids to get information that you don't know they are getting. You want to be the one who decides how your kids hear things," she says.

She recalled how after the Newtown school shooting, a local school district didn't address the issue in its schools at all. Yet, a couple of weeks later they staged lockdown safety drills to prepare in the event of a similar situation within the district.

"If I'm a parent, I want to deliver this message myself. I want to get information from the district on what's going to happen. I don't want my kids to go in there and get blindsided," she explained, adding that some of her child clients came into her office after the Newtown shooting and had no idea it had happened.

"Parents think they can keep it from their kids, but no matter how hard you try, they are going to find out. Families should talk to their kids. Schools should not pretend that it didn't happen. You want children to be prepared in the context of your family values and faith," Masto adds, saying that between social media, news reports, and the age-old school bus or cafeteria chatter, children are likely to get the information parents and other adults are hiding—and they will get that information in a much more frightening and less controlled way. She suggests the best scenario is for schools to plan how to address scary issues and tell parents ahead of time what's going to happen, so that parents can address it at home first and prepare their children for what's coming. Otherwise a safety drill out of context can become a recipe for fear and imaginations run wild.

In an online article posted on TheJournal.ie, clinical psychologist David Trickey says that social media offers both "great potential . . . but also huge risks" for grieving children. "[Once something is posted online] you don't control that information, who knows about it, or who's going to see it and comment on it. People can't help themselves but read the comments. If you tell a friend on the playground that your dad has died, and they say something you don't like, you can turn away. When you're online, you don't get to choose who to edit out."

Trickey echoes Dianna Masto's concerns that no matter how adults may try to shield children from information, the truth always comes out eventually. "A traumatic, sudden death is often reported in the media, and it's going to be online indefinitely. It's better for children to hear it from their family rather than hear it on the playground from their [friends]," says Trickey, adding, "I've never met a child who didn't find out [the truth]. . . . When they're older they will Google the event and learn about it for themselves, and we need to be prepared for that."

Dealing with difficult circumstances

Look at the situation through your child's eyes. How will it change her life? Has she been given enough information to make sense of what's happening? Will this loss change her daily routine? Will it change everything as she knows it? Is she wondering who is going to take care of her or where she is going to live? Is she afraid that something similar is going to happen to her parents, her siblings, or herself? Imagine being a child again and dealing with the loss of someone you love. What would you need most?

Answer questions truthfully, but without gory detail. If a child's grandfather died of cancer and the child was not aware of it prior to the death, now is not the time to talk about the details of the disease. Simply tell the child that Grandpa's heart (liver, lungs, brain) stopped working the way it should. If your child has additional questions, answer them as directly as possible. If a child's sibling died in a car crash, there is no need to talk about everything leading up to the death. Simply talk about the fact that sometimes there are accidents and that the doctors tried to save her brother (sister, father, friend, etc.) but his body was too badly hurt.

Expect new fears to spring from this event and the information you provide. Worries about getting a disease, dying in a car crash, or being in a shooting are likely to surface, depending on the death and the age of your child.

Expect some questions that you will not be able to answer. If a child wants to know why his uncle killed himself, you won't be able to provide a pat answer. The same holds true for other violent deaths that defy logic. When these kinds of questions arise, talk to your child honestly. Don't be afraid to say that you don't have an answer. Contact a support group or clergy member to explore the question and find a resolution to your child's concerns.

Know when to shield children from harmful news that does not affect them directly. Does your child need to hear about every school shooting, every tornado, and every madman who walks into an office building and opens fire? Absolutely not. This is a situation where your child's age can determine what you tell her. If a child is old enough to hear about the event through classmates or newspapers, then by all means talk about it. Use your own judgment and discretion—but if you do choose to discuss an especially alarming death with your child, be prepared to help her wade through the scary information.

Provide one-on-one counseling or group support for your children to help them through their grief. Let children know that it is healthy and beneficial to talk to others, especially professionals, about what they are feeling. If you are grieving as well, you can set a good example by joining a grief support group or seeking a counselor's assistance. Your attitude toward outside help will directly influence your children's attitudes.

Activity: Acting on Your Feelings

We can help children move through grief if we can show them how to turn their inward sorrow into outward action. This is not something you can do with a child who is deep in the initial throes of grief, but rather it is something a child will progress toward as he integrates his feelings of grief into the rest of his life. By becoming an "activist" of sorts, a child will learn how something sad can spark something positive.

Action 1. If a child's deceased loved one was elderly, ask if he would like to volunteer some of his time at a local nursing home or hospital. Visit patients who don't have family around. Sing songs together at the holidays. Read a book to someone who can no longer read for herself. It may take some initial prodding, but it is likely to be an experience he will never forget.

Action 2. Visit a children's ward or children's hospital. Call a hospital and see if it would be OK for your child to bring some colorful balloons, a book for story time, some puppets for a show, or some paper and crayons for arts and crafts. You'll be amazed at how something so simple can be so powerful. Watch the faces light up—theirs and yours!

Action 3. Help a child find an organization dedicated to her loved one's favorite cause or to a cause that is somehow related to his or her death. Encourage her to join a fund-raising walk for AIDS or breast cancer research. Suggest that she volunteer her time with the American Cancer Society, the American Heart Association, the American Diabetes Association, or another appropriate group. Write letters, raise money, donate time.

Action 4. Once a child has worked through some of his own grief issues, see if he would like to become a peer counselor. Many local grief programs train young people to help others their own age.

Action 5. Help a child research topics related to his loved one's death. He may feel empowered by this new information (e.g., using sunblock to ward off skin cancer, eating right to prevent colon cancer, exercising to keep your heart healthy, avoiding cigarettes to prevent lung cancer, knowing the dangers of drinking and driving).

Questions for Reflection

» Has your child experienced an especially traumatic loss? If so, have you been willing to be open and honest, in an age-appropriate way, about what happened? Are you withholding information that could be scary or painful if someone else reveals it to your child without your knowledge?

» Is a tragedy or disaster playing out in the news and on social media right now? Is your child, or a child in your care, likely to hear about it either by chance or because another child or adult unwittingly shares information you were trying to hide? Think about how you can talk to your child about the event in a non-threatening way that reflects your values and your faith.

» Has your child recently learned about the death or terminal illness of a baby or child? If so, have you talked about it? Are you seeing any changes in patterns or behaviors—increased nightmares, trouble sleeping, sudden clinginess, an unwillingness to participate in favorite activities?

» Is your child on social media, or does she have access to the Internet at home, in school, at the public library, or at a friend's house? If so, you can assume that any public event that is playing out anywhere around the world will come across her screen at some point. Can you sit down and talk to your child about the event to prepare her for what she might hear outside of your home?

Meditation: Deepest Sorrows

Abba, Father,
there is nowhere to turn
but to you.
The senseless death,
the heartbreaking suffering
is beyond comprehension,
more than we can bear alone.
Help us to trust
that out of our deepest sorrow
boundless love can grow,
that out of this shattering loss
new life can take root.

7

Respecting a Child's Grief

- Children have a lot to teach us
- Taking things at face value
- The changing landscape of grief
- Don't close the door on their feelings
- What to say, and when to say nothing
- Learning to listen

O divine Master, grant that I may not so much seek to be consoled as to console, to be understood as to understand, to be loved as to love.

—St. Francis of Assisi

Every child experiences death in a unique way. Personality traits, family upbringing, and support systems influence the ways they react. When Gregory Floyd's six-year-old son, John Paul, was hit by a car in front of his house, it set in motion a long journey for Gregory, his wife, Maureen, and their six surviving children. There were good-byes at John Paul's hospital bed, good-byes at the funeral and burial, good-byes as each child came to terms with how their brother's death affected everyday life at home. Through it all, the Floyds were careful to create an environment in which their children felt free to express their feelings.

"We needed to constantly convey to them that there is no such thing as right or wrong feelings, that it's OK to feel angry, to feel sad, to feel happy about Johnny," says Gregory. He recalls how his children would want to paint at an easel, go out for ice cream, and weep for their dead brother all in the span of half an hour.

The Floyds honored their children's feelings and reactions, recognizing that each of them had to grieve in ways that were comfortable. David, who survived being hit by the same car as John Paul, said that he saw his brother "everywhere." No matter where he looked, he had to face his brother's absence. Therese, who Gregory says has a "Miss Fix-It" personality, said at one point that she hated "all this grief." She couldn't deal with the fact that she was unable to make things better. The Floyds' eldest son, Gregory, came to his parents and told them that he felt bad because he didn't have as much sorrow as his mother and father.

"We told him, 'You're not supposed to feel a parent's grief because you're not a parent. You've got a brother-sized grief. You've got enough grief to deal with. You don't need to deal with the grief that Mommy and Daddy are feeling.' He was set free by that."

Children have a lot to teach us

Gregory and Maureen also realized early on that their children were looking to them for cues. They knew they had to exhibit behavior that would allow their children to express their own grief in healthy ways. And, when their own grief took them too deep into themselves, their children were there to pull them back from the depths.

"By being their own vulnerable, charming, needy selves, they helped us immensely," Gregory recalls. "During that first week, I remember standing in the hallway greeting people and mentally feeling like I'm falling off a cliff, and I can't even reach the bottom and crash. I'm just free-falling endlessly. Then I feel this little tug on my thigh from my daughter Susanna, and I get called back to life because there's a little child here who needs me. That was how God used them to draw us out of ourselves, because children are essentially needy."

He says that "obedience to the everyday"—getting the kids dressed, making them breakfast, saying their prayers with them, and tucking them in at night—forced the family to move forward. The same can be true for anyone dealing with grief. A return to "normal" life helps take children away from their grief for brief moments throughout the day. A routine provides a framework. If their daily needs are being met—food, clothes, sleep, comfort—children are more likely to begin to heal emotionally and spiritually. And by staying involved in their daily routines, we put ourselves in the position of being available to them whenever a scary thought or question comes up.

Parents and other adult caregivers can take their cues from children when they are grieving the death of someone close to them. We can respect their feelings, accept their reactions, and encourage their healing. By putting aside our preconceived notions of what grief should be like, we allow children to become our teachers. With our permission, they will open up to us, trust us, and maybe even help us a little along the way.

My sister-in-law, Alison Martin, now in her twenties, was only ten years old when she came across a story in *Good Housekeeping* about a one-year-old boy who suffocated after getting tangled in his crib sheet. Although it affected her deeply, she initially didn't say anything to her parents about it. In a conversation a few weeks later, she mentioned something to her mother about sheets being dangerous. My mother-in-law, Mary Ann Poust, says that at first she scoffed at the idea, but Alison said she would prove her point and came back with the article in hand.

"I was surprised at what I read, but more surprised at her interest and knowledge," noted Mary Ann. "That opened the discussions as to how badly she felt for that family and how sad she was that the child had died. To help her feel that she could help in some way, I suggested that she write to the mother expressing sympathy and making a contribution to the foundation they had set up."

Alison did just that, making a twenty-five-dollar donation that would go toward a playground the family was building at the public school their little boy would have attended. But it didn't end there. Alison and the child's mother continued to correspond from time to time, and Alison even made a presentation on the crib sheet issue at her school. When the playground was dedicated in June 1999, Alison and her parents made the drive from Manhattan to Norwood, Massachusetts, for the event. The family even singled out Alison during the event, telling everyone there how much she had helped the grieving mother.

Mary Ann thinks the situation had such a dramatic impact on Alison because it made her realize that sometimes bad things happen even when you're in a situation that's considered safe. "The baby was in his own home, his own room, and his own bed," she says. "His mother was in the house, taking care of him. And yet he died. Although she never articulated it in that way, I think that was an awakening for Alison, and a frightening one. I think her activism was a way of dealing with it."

And so there we have a perfect example of how a child can be moved to great lengths by the death of someone she doesn't even know. Her parents could have told her to forget about it. They could have said it was sad but not her problem. They certainly could have said that it was too far to drive to another state for a playground dedication. But they didn't. They honored their daughter's feelings, and she responded by moving through her initial reaction to a place where she could use her concern to comfort a mother in grief and educate others. That is what can happen when parents watch, listen, and learn.

Taking things at face value

Michaelene Mundy, a teacher, mother, counselor, and author, believes that parents and other adults can look for the "simple insights" children offer into how they understand death and grief. If we are awake to those insights, we can take them to the next level by helping children find the answers to their questions.

"Children deserve our respect," Mundy says. "My main admonition to parents, teachers, and caregivers is to communicate—that doesn't mean just talk, but listen carefully to what a child is saying. Children are very literal, so it's important to be aware of what we say to our children. They are listening to what is said around them and are interpreting in the best way they know how with their limited experience."

Mundy recalls that when her son Michael was three years old, he believed her deceased father lived in the attic. He had heard her speak of someone being "up in heaven" and also understood that heaven was not a place you could visit. In his preschool mind he put two and two together: The entrance to the attic was a square hole "up" in the ceiling. Nobody ever went there, but he knew it existed. In his mind, that was where his grandfather must be.

Think about even the most basic ways children can misinterpret what we say. I can remember times when my children were young and would misunderstand something we adults took for granted. Saying that we were going to "throw" a load of wash in or "run" to the store would get a child's mind whirring. "The store is too far away," Noah would respond when he was preschool age, and I would end up in a ridiculously long discussion about the simplest things, or, at least, simple to me. The same holds true for children who are trying to understand death. A statement that seems simple to us can suggest strange concepts and images to a child.

Father Terence Curley, a grief expert and the author of *The Ministry of Consolation: A Parish Guide for Comforting the Bereaved*, says that euphemisms and attempts to shield children from the truth can add to a child's emotional confusion.

"Our language is important in the way we talk about death with the child," says Father Curley. "Children can easily misinterpret our abstractions. For example, telling a child that someone was so good that God took them could bring about real problems. In the child's view this could mean that if you're really good God is going to take you too. This can be frightening and certainly shapes the child's image of God." The key is honesty. The truth is always best, no matter how painful.

The changing landscape of grief

In the beginning, a child's grief can seem overwhelming for parents and caregivers to deal with. But remember that this, too, will pass, though it will not pass quickly. Just as we cannot teach children all there is to know about right and wrong in one night, we cannot hope to explain death, grief, mourning, resurrection, and survival in one sitting. Over the months and years ahead, questions will continue to come up. This is normal and healthy. Experts call it "regrieving," but for most of us it's simply called life.

A child's graduation comes along, and he thinks about how his mom would have been so proud. A daughter prepares to get married, and she cries because her dad is not there to walk her down the aisle. Over and over again, children who have suffered a loss will be reminded of it, saddened by it, and affected by it in new ways. This grief is never as intense as the early grief, but it is grief nonetheless, and it is important to honor and respect it.

Gregory Floyd has seen that as each year goes by, the horrible images of his son lying unconscious on the front lawn become more muted, and the images of John Paul happy and laughing become more vibrant. However, he fully expects his children to "revisit" their grief at different moments in their lives.

"While life moves on and is full of good things, we will have moments of this reality piercing our awareness as well as our hearts until the day we die," he states. "I have no doubt about that whatsoever. It doesn't mean that life isn't happy. It means that it's happy, plus there will be piercing moments."

My own grief over my mother's death resurfaced when I had my children. It was most dramatic when Noah was born, because he was my first, and I had so many questions that could not be answered. I wanted my mother to be there to tell me about her experiences as a new mother. I was angry over what I perceived as the injustice of it all. My child was missing a grandparent, and I could never convey to him what she was truly like. When Olivia came along three and a half years later, I grieved again but in a different way. I was more melancholy. The acceptance came more readily, and that made everything that much sadder. And my experience with grief at Chiara's birth another five years later was different still. How was it possible that I had gotten used to the absence of my mother? Even as an adult, that realization can take you aback.

Those feelings can be even stronger for a child who lost a parent before he had any conscious memories of their time together. When he regrieves later in life, there are no happy images to conjure up, no words of wisdom to fill the clanging void. For these children, it is especially important for surviving parents, siblings, grandparents, extended family and friends, and other caring adults to do all they can to forge a connection to the deceased parent.

If a child is only three years old when her mother dies, then it is up to the survivors to make that parent a kind of presence in the child's future. Through pictures, stories, and memorials, that child can have happy memories to fall back on as she grows and reflects on her mother's death in more mature ways.

As I recalled at the beginning of this book, I was only five years old when my grandfather died. I talked about him pushing me in a swing hanging from his willow tree and about his relentless teasing. At this point, I don't know if those are real memories or memories that were created after years and years of hearing those happy stories. For me it doesn't really matter. They are part of my consciousness and help me remember my grandfather fondly.

Don't close the door on their feelings

Sometimes children will amaze us with their perceptiveness, their understanding, and their ability to withstand adult-sized emotions despite their child-sized frames. If we allow children to be themselves and are willing to look for signs of sorrow and listen to their expressions of sadness, we just might be surprised by a child's resiliency and strength.

Kathy Duke says that because of her son's experiences with his sister Emma's death, and the death of other friends at the Ronald McDonald House where they stayed during Emma's illness, he understands that sometimes children die. "By the time Joseph was six years old he had witnessed a tremendous amount of loss. I have to give a lot of credit to him. He has always been really good at articulating his feelings, and he has not suppressed them," she says.

Although Kathy doesn't want to take any credit for Joe's healthy journey through grief, she should. She talks with Joe about Emma whenever they see something that reminds them of her. Two years after her death, they were still hanging Emma's stocking up at Christmas. They managed to remember Emma without getting pulled down by their grief.

"She's just still a part of us. I think that helps Joe—it certainly helps us—because we don't want to act like it never happened. I have had a lot of people tell me that they are amazed at how open and articulate Joe is about his feelings. One time he came home from kindergarten just months after Emma died with a picture that had a rainbow at the top. It was supposed to be whatever you wish for, and it said, 'I wish my sister could come back.'"

Joe is lucky because his mother was willing to let him say what needed to be said and to remember his sister at Christmas or any other time her memory popped into his head. Other children are not always so fortunate. We adults sometimes hide our own emotions and, without realizing it, make children think they shouldn't express their feelings either.

Often children will take the lead in discussing their emotions when the adults around them will not. The Dougy Center in Portland, Oregon, was established in response to a young boy's desperate attempt to find someone willing to talk to him about his impending death. His name, of course, was Dougy, and he had an inoperable brain tumor. He wrote a letter to death-and-dying expert Elisabeth Kübler Ross asking why adults wouldn't talk to him about the fact that he knew he was dying. She wrote back and sent him a little booklet that is now called "A Letter to a Child with Cancer" or "The Dougy Letter." Dougy took it around to the other kids at the hospital and decided that if the adults wouldn't talk to them, they'd talk to one another. A nurse at the hospital was so impressed by how Dougy got the other children to open up that she decided to start a program to help kids deal with terminal illness or the death of someone they love. That program grew into the Dougy Center.

Donna Schuurman, executive director of the Dougy Center, suggests that most problems stem from our fear of death and our fear of not knowing what to say to children. Often we can't deal with a child's pain or don't think it's healthy to dwell on the matter, so we pressure our children to "get over" their grief quickly. "There are some parallels to sex education," Schuurman says. "Often what happens is nothing. People think kids will figure it out. We make it into a big deal, and it wouldn't have to be if it were incorporated naturally and not avoided."

What to say, and when to say nothing

It's never easy to know exactly what to say when a child is in crisis. We usually feel our way along. Too often I slip into a preachy mode when I'm talking to Chiara, my youngest, about something serious, or I digress and lose her—and my point—along the way. When it comes to helping grieving children, less is more.

Peter Assumma, funeral director of Assumma-Shankey Funeral Home in Pearl River, New York, says that if we could look at life and death as a child does, we would find the subject very simple and very real. "Most of the questions children have are very basic. Parents get flustered because they are not listening to the questions," he says.

For instance, a child's grandmother dies, and that grandmother always made the child soup. Upon hearing of his beloved grandma's death, the child's only comment may be, "Who is going to make me soup now?" The parents, reeling from their own grief and unable to understand how their child could be thinking about soup, begin to talk about death and angels and heaven.

"The kid wants to know who's making the soup," explains Assumma. "He wants to know who's going to feed him and clothe him."

It helps if we can hold our tongue and let children speak, being careful to convey to them through our body language, eye contact, and tone that we are interested in, and open to, what they are saying. Turn toward them, speak in a normal tone and at a normal speed, and let your face reflect your empathy and concern. I remember how my son, still a preschooler, would say, "Why do you have that face on, Mom?" when I was talking about a serious subject with him. It immediately brought me out of whatever was troubling me and reminded me to lighten up. Kids notice things like that, so we adults need to be aware of them as well.

We also don't want to get to a point where we're finishing a child's thoughts, interrupting his, or telling him what he's feeling. We have to give children whatever time they need to tell us in their own way what's happening. When that's done, then we can restate what they've said to let them know that we heard and understood them. For example, "It sounds as though you're really angry about your grandpa's death. Is that right?"

We can also phrase questions in ways that will encourage children to open up rather than simply reply with a yes or no answer. "Do you want to join a grief support group to help you deal with your anger?" will not do as much for a child as "What might we do to help you deal with this anger?" The first question forces the child into a decision. The second question allows him to talk about his feelings and maybe come up with a solution of his own, which will be empowering in and of itself.

Sometimes kids will say nothing at all. That's when parents are most likely to start talking and asking a lot of questions—we feel a need to fill the void. We want to get to the bottom of the problem. Sometimes that means doing nothing. If children are not ready to talk, our pushing and prodding will probably only make things worse. That doesn't mean we should ignore or abandon them. It does mean we should find a way to coexist with the silence. Suggest an outing to a park or try cooking a favorite meal together, or, if we're an adult caregiver, an activity or game. Working together—even in silence—may be enough to make a child relax and open up.

Learning to listen

It's important for a child to feel that she can express any and all emotions, as long as those expressions do not hurt her or anyone else. Expect some pretty strong reactions from children who are experiencing the loss of a family member. Anger, sadness, denial, fear, withdrawal—all of these reactions come with the territory. Don't give in to your urge to put a lid on it. Allow your child the freedom to go where she needs to go emotionally. That being said, don't allow your child to spiral downward into a dangerous emotional hole where rage or depression or fantasy becomes the new reality. Provide ample room for a child's emotions but be ready to step in with the safety net of your adult experience, care, and love when those emotions get too big for her to handle.

Validate feelings by acknowledging that they are normal. Sometimes kids need only to hear that their fear, anger, sadness, confusion, or guilt is normal. Let them witness some of your emotions. Don't pretend you're not angry or sad just to protect your children. Simply telling your children that it's OK to feel sad or scared or mad is often enough to let them release their feelings.

Expect children to approach grief in different ways. No two children will experience a death the same way. Some will want to talk about their deceased loved one; others will retreat to a place of silence for a while. Every child is unique, as is every family. How your children respond to a loss will depend on how they respond to things in general and how your family handles crises of any kind. Does everyone work themselves up into a frenzy? Do you hold a family meeting to talk and pray? Do the parents pit themselves against one another? Do the children get cut out of meaningful discussions? All of these things will influence how children grieve. Try to keep them in the loop. Don't allow anger or sadness to separate you from your children.

Expect children to "regrieve" throughout their lives. Any significant loss a child experiences will be with him forever—at least in some ways. Although the initial mind-numbing grief will pass with time, a less virulent form of grief will probably remain for years and years. Be prepared for it as major milestones approach: anniversaries, birthdays, favorite holidays, graduations, marriages, births, illnesses, and deaths. It is not unusual for children to experience milder forms of grief at any or all of these occasions.

Activity: Replacing Bad Memories

Pastoral counselor Dorothy Armstrong encourages parents and adult caregivers to help children move through their grief by helping them "reframe" the pictures that may flash through their minds. Perhaps the only image a child has of his deceased father is that of him on his deathbed, or at his wake. That image can keep a child trapped emotionally in one place for a long time. We don't want children to forget things that happened, but we do want them to replace the continuous loop of negative images with more positive ones.

"Children are so good at this," says Armstrong, who is also trained in neuro-linguistic programming. "You want to help your child in grief to reframe a memory so that the same painful picture doesn't keep playing over and over."

Step 1. Ask your child to think about the memory or picture that comes to mind whenever he thinks of his deceased loved one. Is it happy, sad, frightening? Is that image keeping him from doing other things?

Step 2. Now start talking to your child about the happiest memory he has of his loved one. Is it a special vacation they took together, nightly bedtime stories they read, trips to the library they took each week, warm hugs they shared before heading out to school and work each day?

Step 3. Tell your child to try to turn off the sad "video" that has been playing in his mind. Put this new, happy memory in its place and let it be the image that appears instead. By changing the way a child pictures a scene, we can change his emotions and even a bit of his history. Watching videos or looking through photo albums to catch a glimpse of a loved one laughing and enjoying himself can help a child recapture some happy images.

Step 4. Recognize that it may take time for your child to reach a point where he is able to do this. It is only normal for him to focus on his sorrowful memories for a certain period of time. Eventually it will become easier to push the sad memories out of the way to make room for happier thoughts. It can help to do things that bring back happy thoughts of the child's loved one—bake her favorite cookie recipe, listen to her favorite music, rent her favorite movie. Find a way to recall the joy she found in simple things, and see if your child can grab some of that joy for himself.

Questions for Reflection

» Are you taking cues from your grieving child or trying to force him to grieve the way you would grieve? Stop talking and just watch and listen for a while; see if you can't pick up some clues as to what your child is feeling and thinking.

» Do you use phrases or words that could confuse a child and give him an inaccurate or even scary view of something related to his deceased loved one, death in general, heaven, or God?

» Think about your child's grief process to date. What have been the hardest times? Where have you seen the most growth or progress?

» Is your child still in the early days of grief? If so, expect all of the "firsts" to be especially difficult—birthdays, holidays, anniversaries, and special events such as graduations or first communion. Is your child more removed from the initial grief? If so, expect regrieving to occur whenever special days and events surface, even well into adulthood.

Meditation: Grief Maps

Grief does not move in a straight line.
It twists and turns and bends back on itself,
taking us to places we'd rather not go.
Day by day with care and prayer
we inch forward in slowly fading sorrow,
until we eventually catch a glimpse
of a new version of our old self,
of a life changed but worth living,
of a joy that while tinged with sadness
is enough to carry us home.

8

The Role of Faith in Healthy Grieving

- Understanding a child's faith perspective
- Questioning, doubting God
- Explaining heaven, even when we can't
- The special needs of teenagers
- Nurturing faith before grief hits

I am the resurrection and the life. Those who believe in me,
even though they die, will live.
—John 11:25

Faith may not get us through our grief any faster, but it certainly can make the journey a lot less harrowing. If parents have passed onto their children a belief in resurrection and eternal life, then they, too, will have something to turn to in their sorrow. That doesn't mean that children won't question God's wisdom or even accuse God of taking revenge on them by stealing away a loved one. All those reactions are normal. In fact, parents go through many of the same emotions. But in the end, faith offers a kind of support that cannot be found anywhere else.

Father Terence Curley, president of the National Catholic Bereavement Ministry and author of several books on loss and grief, says that faith during grief is crucial. "I don't think faith is something added on; it is essential for the grieving process. It's the way in which we bring some meaning out of all the chaos. Faith and trust are synonymous and with a child, you can almost use the two words interchangeably."

It's best if we parents can reflect on our own beliefs before uttering a word to our children. Do we feel confident telling our children their grandma is with God? Do we really believe death is just another part of life? Do we believe our deceased loved one is still watching over us and that we will see her again? Once we come to terms with those questions, we can talk to our children about trust, love, hope, and the belief that one day we will be reunited with our loved ones in heaven.

These same principles hold true for other important adults in a child's life. Whether parent or caregiver, if we have an influential role in a child's day-to-day routine, our beliefs will inevitably come into play when we are talking to children about their beliefs, especially during times of crisis.

"Hopefully, the role of religion is to tie the whole thing together," says Father Curley. "As a vehicle for children, it is an essential one because in our faith we want to teach them early on that life isn't taken away; life is changed. The whole idea is that you take a child's loss and place it in the context of faith or in the context of our trust in God. To do anything else would be to do a disservice to the whole experience of life for the child."

Understanding a child's faith perspective

A child's faith begins forming from early infancy. The baby who feels secure with his parents and trusts that they will keep him from harm begins to sense the love of a more powerful being. As a child grows and becomes more aware of the world around him, he realizes that his parents are separate from himself and that God is totally other. At about this time, children begin to use their imaginations to form pictures of God. Before long, they weave together what they have been taught, what they have overheard, and what they have imagined.

Michael Brown, director of Spiritual Care at Mayo Clinic Health System–Franciscan Healthcare in La Crosse, Wisconsin, says that the best time to talk to children about death and resurrection is before the crisis hits. "Ask what they think happens when you die. Where do they think they came from? What do they think heaven is like? Where is God? Get them to tell you what they think, because in a way they already have some knowledge."

It helps if we can get past our own fears about death and talk honestly to children about our faith. "It's a matter of accepting death as a normal part of life. Children shouldn't be shielded from that," Brown states.

Think about the last time you grieved for someone or something that disappeared from your life. There was probably a pain at the

144 Parenting a Grieving Child

very center of your being, the feeling that the heartache would never subside.

When I lost a baby through miscarriage, I sat down in the shower one day and cried at the top of my lungs while the water poured over my head. I cried because of my sadness, I cried out in anger with God, and I cried for the baby I would never know. At the time I thought I would never feel whole again. Grief can be like that. It can leave us aching inside.

Children are no different. No one can take those feelings of sorrow away from a grieving child, and no one should try. We each have a right to grieve, to mourn, and to let the sadness pour over us, at least to a point.

Dorothy Armstrong, a New Jersey-based pastoral counselor who works with people in grief, has seen that most people do not want to be denied their time in grief. "To miss someone I loved—that has a divine flavor. Jesus loved Lazarus and groaned at his tomb because he wanted him alive. That pain in one's heart—that is not a bad thing, as long as it's life-giving," she says. "When you love people and you miss them, then that is a very beautiful pain. It reaches a point in our innermost beings, in the depths of our faith. That's a pain that I don't want to be totally deprived of, the pain of love."

Children have a natural affinity for spirituality that is strengthened by the beliefs that have been incorporated into their lives, Armstrong says. "We have this very dynamic faith. Even children can talk about heaven, and they grasp it so easily."

Questioning, doubting God

For adults and children alike, feeling abandoned by God can be the ultimate feeling of loneliness. We look to God for protection, for the answers to our prayers. When something devastating happens, we wonder how God could allow—or even cause—this tragedy. It can shake our faith, and it can leave us feeling as though we have to go through this difficult journey alone.

Jennifer Morgan questioned her faith in the wake of her fourteen-year-old brother's death. "We went to church as a family every weekend, and we were sent to Catholic schools. How could God do this to us? . . . At my Catholic high school, God was at the core of our school. I secretly hated God for what he did. Later when I left for college, I chose not to attend church—not until my senior year. One of the classes I chose for my psychology minor was on death and dying. I not only found myself learning about the subject but also growing spiritually."

Jennifer's mother, Lorraine Wilson, remembers her own faith crisis after Robby's death. She continued to take the children to Mass on Sunday despite her own doubts and anger.

"In the beginning, faith is very important. It gets you through," says Lorraine. "Then, as reality sets in, you realize that you lost a child and he's not coming back. You get very angry with God. We still went to church because of the children. Sometimes I would just sit in church and look at Jesus on the cross and think about the fact that Mary went through this. She lost her son, and I am certainly no better than her. I got angry with God, but then my faith returned. I am a firm believer that I am going to be reunited with Robby."

Witnessing a strong belief in God—especially in times of crisis or sorrow—can serve grieving children well. They learn that even in the midst of doubt and anger and sadness, they can talk to God. They learn that it's normal to question their faith and that, when all is said and done, they can rely on and return to their beliefs.

Regis Flaherty, a former cemetery director, saw the power of faith firsthand in his dealings with grieving families over three decades. He has often been privy to their innermost emotions and beliefs. What he has seen has convinced him that faith provides comfort to adults and children alike.

"Parents have to try to give children a concept of resurrection, that life is not being ended but changed. It's important for parents to understand those faith issues and have a way to communicate them," he says. "Try to convey to the child your belief that we continue to help those who have died through prayer, that we believe they are with Jesus, and that in the resurrection we will be reunited to them again."

Praying for the dead can be a blessing. All these years later, I remember saying my childhood bedtime prayers and including "Grandpa in heaven." Now my own children say the same bedtime prayers and include their "Grandma in heaven." It helps keep her memory alive. It helps to know that we can still connect to her in some way.

We can teach children to remember loved ones and friends not only at bedtime but also during Mass or on special feast days, holy days, or anniversaries. We can simply mention their names or we can say more formal prayers. Either way, the power of prayer cannot be overestimated.

Explaining heaven, even when we can't

The idea among adults that children are too young to understand spiritual issues is nothing new. After all, Jesus had to admonish his followers, saying, "Let the children come to me." We adults often think like those early disciples. Maybe it's because we are dealing with our own faith issues, or maybe we just don't realize how deeply children have been touched by the spiritual lessons they have been taught.

Gregory Floyd witnessed his own children's deep spirituality both before and after their brother's death. "You can talk to children about heaven and about the deep realities of life," he says. "We radically underestimate the spirituality of children. They latch onto things, not with the depth of an adult, but sometimes in their very simplicity they transcend some of the things that the adults are struggling with."

When I was writing the first edition of this book years ago, Noah was a preschooler. Even after months and months of research and writing on this topic, I still cringed a bit when he asked me about heaven and I had to explain things. Did I pick the right words and the right images? We talked about heaven and how it is the place we will go after we die, the place where we will be with God and with people who have already died. We talked about the fact that it's not anything we can see or anything we can really know because no one on earth has ever seen it.

"Is heaven in outer space?" Noah asked, looking up at the planets and stars suspended from his bedroom ceiling. We talked a little more about how heaven is beyond outer space, beyond anything we can imagine. Years later, his little sister, Chiara, who often reminds me of her big brother, asked similar questions about heaven.

"What does heaven mean?" she asked me, when she was only three. And I explained in much the same way I had explained it a decade before. Chiara followed it up not by asking a question but by making a statement: "E-ma is very old. E-ma is never going to die." E-ma, our nickname for my Italian grandmother, was ninety-six at the time. I explained to her that E-ma would, in fact, die one day and we would be sad, and this is how the conversation continued:

Chiara: "And she will find God?"

Me: "Or God will find her."

Chiara: "Who else is going to die except for E-ma?"

Me: "We're all going to die. Every living thing has to die. But hopefully that will not come until we are very old."

Chiara: "So everyone except for us is going to die."

Me: "Um, no. We'll die too someday, but hopefully a long, long time from now. Hopefully not until we get old like E-ma."

Chiara: "And we will see God, but our house will still be here, right?"

Me: "Right."

Chiara (climbing onto my lap): "I don't want to die. It's not coming yet, right?"

I had always assumed that Noah's fascination with death and heaven had something to do with my work on this book at the time. I figured I had unwittingly passed on what I was writing about or had used him as a grief guinea pig one too many times. As it turns out, this is just normal operating procedure for many children, especially if they are being raised in a home where topics like heaven and resurrection and prayers are standard fare.

Chiara kept coming back to our conversation throughout that day, asking if I was old or if she was old, trying to get some sort of guarantee that, as she put it, "it's not coming yet." If only we could make such guarantees. I have to admit that I lingered a little longer than usual when I tucked her in that night. I wished I could give her the answer she was looking for, just as I had wished I could give Noah the answer he was looking for all those years before. We can't necessarily give children the definitive answer they'd like or the fairytale ending we all want, but we can be present and we can answer honestly from our own place of faith and our hope in all that is to come.

Chaplain Michael Brown states that the key to discussing faith issues with children is to be realistic about their developmental stage. "It doesn't really do any good to start quoting Scripture or start trying to teach doctrine to a four-year-old. That's not the way they understand the world. You need to talk to children about faith and get them to tell you the stories they weave together."

So how do we tell a young child what happens to us after we die? We can simply explain what we believe: that our soul continues to live, that we will see our loved one again in heaven, that God promised us a place in heaven with him for all time. If a child is old enough to know more about the life of Jesus, we can rely on more explicit stories from Scripture about how Jesus taught us that there would be no more death.

If children are too young to grasp the idea that a person's body is no longer thinking or feeling, we can offer a more concrete example of why the body is not needed after death.

"Compare it to something in a box," Chaplain Brown suggests. "When you take the things out, you no longer need the box. That's not exactly theologically correct, but we're not dealing with cognitive stuff. You just want to help children understand that this person isn't suffering. They're not feeling sad. They don't feel cold. They're not asleep. Their body isn't working at all, and the person no longer needs that body. God has given them a new one. We will see them again in that new body when we have died and we have received our new bodies."

The special needs of teenagers

Because teens are desperately trying to develop their individuality, talking to them about faith in the midst of grief can be a lesson in futility. They often reject whatever their parents say, and lessons in faith are no exception. Although we parents should continue to set limits, it's best to do so knowing that children must go through this teen phase in order to emerge as healthy, independent adults.

Michael Brown says that what's most important to a teen at this point in her faith and grief is not what we say but what we do. "Kids at this age are very much into faith in action," he says. "They're also going to be very justice-minded about it when somebody close to them dies. They're going to say, 'Look, you always told me God is a loving God. Why did God take this person?' You're not going to be able to answer that question simply, and it's kind of futile to try because the teenager has a point. You've got to be able to say, 'I don't know.'"

Teens are likely to feel angry about death and will be thrown off when a crisis challenges whatever image they may still have of a warm and loving God. "It's going to shake that to its roots, and it's not going to be resolved in one conversation," says Brown.

Teens will watch to see how the adults around them are working through their own questions about death and faith. What we as parents and adult caregivers can do is give them a positive example, be willing to talk about difficult issues, and let them have their opinions.

Nurturing faith before grief hits

Nobody wants to think that they're going to need to sit down with a child and talk about death. We like to convince ourselves that this topic isn't relevant to our lives, and it might not be—at least not right now. But it will be, if not today then someday down the road or maybe even tomorrow.

If we have to start laying a foundation of faith in the midst of intense grieving, it makes everything more complicated. Suddenly children are facing the concept of life after death, perhaps for the first time, while they also are grappling with the loss of a parent or grandparent or sibling or friend. It helps if we can give children the building blocks of faith from their earliest days so they have something to hold onto when death and loss send them reeling.

Get the lay of the land. Start by asking children or teens what they believe about God, Jesus, and heaven. They may know more than you realize, or they may be working with a patched-together version of faith that does them more harm than good. Let them explain their faith in their own words so you have a starting point.

Start with the basics. If a child hasn't been raised in the faith, begin with the most basic elements. Use stories from Scripture to introduce key concepts and figures such as God the Father, Holy Spirit, Jesus,

Mary, and Joseph. Expand to other important figures when you feel a child is ready.

Present life as a circle. Talk about death, resurrection, Easter, eternal life, and what we believe about heaven. If we can talk to children about these subjects before they have to apply them to a loved one who has just died, we can take some of the fear and confusion out of it.

Keep the conversation going. Ask them if they have any questions. Be prepared for anything, from questions about angels and hell to doubts about resurrection and heaven. If you can't answer a question, don't be afraid to tell your child that you need to look something up or get more information to explain it properly. In fact, you could choose to find the answers to the questions together, allowing the child to take ownership of his faith and his beliefs.

Seek outside support. If a child is not already enrolled in either Catholic school or a parish faith formation program, call your church to inquire about how to register for classes.

Activity: A Time and Place for Prayer

When we think about prayer, we don't have to limit our images to kneeling in a pew at church. A prayer can be a long walk with your child in the crisp evening air. Watch the moon rising, breathe deeply of God's goodness, look at the stars, and talk about things you see along the way. Anything and everything we do can become a prayer. In fact, our lives would be so much happier if we could all approach every day that way. When we are in grief, prayer is even more important. Here are some suggestions for bringing God into your home and your life.

Begin by simply making room for God— in your consciousness, in your schedule, and in your home. That doesn't mean you have to carry around a prayer book or spend every afternoon saying the Rosary with your children. It means learning to find God in the ordinary events of the day—in line at the drive-in window at the bank, walking your child across the parking lot before school, in the silence before a roaring fire.

Set aside regular times to pray, times that your child will come to expect and anticipate—in the morning, before dinner, at bedtime. You can rely on favorite prayers that you remember from your childhood or experiment with creating prayers of your own.

Teach your child to talk to God. Don't simply recite a laundry list of wishes, but rather learn to express your sorrows, joys, and fears. A child will begin to see God as a friend, someone who will listen to her troubles when she is lying awake at night.

Create a special place to pray— around a small table in the living room, kneeling next to your child's bed, or hands joined around the kitchen table. Add candles, a statue or cross, flowers, an inspiring quote for reflection, and perhaps a photo of your deceased loved one or some other remembrance. Silence the television, radio, stereo, and all phones during times of prayer.

Go to church and let your child light a candle in your loved one's memory. Kneel down together in prayer.

Arrange to have Mass offered in your loved one's name. Attend with your child, and then do something together afterward.

Questions for Reflection

» If your child, or a child in your care, is grieving right now, how strong is her foundation of faith? Has she been taught to believe in life after death, heaven, and eternal life?

» Are your children expressing doubts about God or anger toward God? These are normal reactions, especially where teens are concerned. Can you give your child room to let out his feelings, even if you find them upsetting or uncomfortable?

» The concepts of heaven, resurrection, and eternal life can be difficult for adults to comprehend, and even more so for children. What do you believe about these subjects and other key beliefs? Reflecting on your own faith will help you support children who may be thinking about their faith in a deep way for the first time.

» How can you weave prayer into your child's life so that he begins to see it as a way to talk to God when he is upset, worried, or afraid? What everyday moments or activities might lend themselves to times of shared prayer between you and your child?

Meditation: World without End

We believe in your promise, God,
even when sorrow makes us
question what it all means.
Give us courage when we
are starting to doubt.
Give us comfort when we
are feeling alone in the world.
Give us strength when we
are struggling to face another day
without our loved one beside us.

9

Rituals of Faith Offer Comfort, Healing, Memories

- The role of rituals
- Is a child ever too young to attend a funeral?
- Preparing children for a wake or funeral
- Involving children to make meaningful memories
- Graveside services, cremation, and the grieving process
- Helping children see cemeteries as sacred, not scary
- Preparing for a wake

Rituals remind us that life is eternal.
—Terence P. Curley, *Six Steps for Managing Loss*

Pink crepe myrtle blossoms hang overhead as dozens of people gather on the shores of the Colorado River. A little boy in a burnt orange Texas Longhorns T-shirt clutches a bouquet of pink and yellow gerbera daisies with a profound sense of seriousness. A teenage boy in baggy jeans nonchalantly twirls a solemn long-stem rose between his thin fingertips. A young girl in a frilly, cream-colored lace dress kneels down in the parched grass to touch a name on a stone marker.

Under a cloudless blue October sky, the children and their families look at a map to find "their" trees, marked with heart-shaped name tags along the river that is known as Lady Bird Lake in downtown Austin, Texas. They are searching for the trees they have donated in memory of deceased parents and grandparents, brothers and sisters, friends and relatives. They are searching for a way to bring some closure and some peace to their lives after the devastation of death and grief.

While the adults shake hands, wipe away tears, and offer hugs to one another, the children find their own ways to cope. They watch the birds flying overhead, find a thick tree limb to climb, follow the path of a cyclist on the nearby hike-and-bike trail, twirl a white rose like a weightless baton. This ceremony is as much for them as it is for the adults, and they trail their families up to the podium to accept certificates and hear the names of the deceased read out in a roll call that is at once full of sorrow and full of hope.

A young girl armed with a disposable camera points and clicks, capturing for posterity—and perhaps for comfort on the long road to healing—a mother's name carved in stone, a fragile sapling blowing in the autumn breeze, a celebration that insists that death will not have the last word.

The role of rituals

If you take ritual and ceremony out of life, you take away so much of the stuff that gives us our memories and allows us to hold onto events that might otherwise fade from our mind's eye. From the baptism that celebrates new life to the anointing of the sick that signals preparation for death, our lives move to the rhythm of rituals that not only impart meaning but also leave indelible marks on our hearts.

Remember the way your first communion dress puffed out when you sat down in the pew, the way your high-school ring caught the sunlight as you accepted your diploma, the way the church smelled of gardenias when you walked down the aisle to get married? The major milestones of our lives serve as the bookmarks that allow us to turn back to earlier chapters and relive a particular day, if only for a fleeting moment.

Death and grief and mourning require the same attention to ritual, especially for children who often have no other way to cope with the loss of a beloved relative or friend. Most of us seek the closure and finality that come from attending a funeral or throwing dirt on a casket as it is lowered into the ground. Adults often think that children do not want or need such stark reminders of their loss, but the truth is that they do need the opportunity to participate in ceremonies or create rituals of their own. It is a way for them to bookmark the life and death of their deceased loved one so that it can be looked up, relived, mourned, or celebrated whenever there is a longing or a need.

Is a child ever too young to attend a funeral?

Mention the subject of children and funerals, and inevitably the question comes up: can a child be too young to attend a wake, funeral, burial, or memorial service? As adults who have weathered and, in many cases, assimilated the death-denying precepts of our society, it is only logical that we project our views and feelings onto the children in our lives. We assume that the sight of Grandma lying in a casket draped with flowers cannot possibly be healthy for someone so young.

In reality, however, young children are often more adept than adults at handling the difficult aspects of death. Seeing the peaceful smile on Grandma's face, saying good-bye one last time, and dropping a note or a favorite trinket into the casket as a reminder of the happy times are ways for children to reconcile Grandma's absence from the dinner table with the abstract explanation of death that Mom and Dad gave them before walking into the funeral home.

Funeral director Peter Assumma encourages parents to take their children to a funeral home for an informal visit, in much the same way they might take them to the fire station or the library. "If we expose our children to death, then that's the only way they are going to have a full understanding of life. When folks ask about bringing kids in, I tell them that I can guarantee they won't have a problem. I tell them that if the kids are crying, it is usually because they are picking up on the adults' moods."

Assumma, who has worked in the funeral industry for more than thirty years, turned the smoking lounge in his funeral home into a playroom for children. They can watch videos, play games, make noise, and let off steam when sitting still in the viewing room upstairs gets to be too much for them.

It is not always easy, however, to convince us parents that children may benefit from attending a wake or funeral. Often we are so caught up in our own sorrow that we forget that our children have to accept and process the death as well. With or without our encouragement, children will find ways to cope with death, but it is the job of parents and other responsible adults to help them cope in the healthiest ways possible.

Assumma invites parents to bring children to the funeral home before the public viewing, so he can talk with them, answer questions, and allow them to view their loved one in private. Most questions younger children have at the viewing are basic ones. They want to know how Grandpa feels lying in the casket. Can he hear? Can he hurt? Will he wake up? Because caskets with only the top half open are the norm, Assumma says many children are afraid that the deceased person's legs have been chopped off. He makes a point of lifting the bottom half of the casket lid so that children can see the whole body, and even touch the legs if they like.

I witnessed that curiosity firsthand when my niece's great-grandmother died. Kaci was only four years old at the time, and my sister carefully explained what she would see when she got to the funeral home and told her that she did not have to get close to the casket if she did not want to. Once at the funeral home, however, Kaci could not stay away from the casket. She kept finding reasons to walk past it, to peer over the edge. She went out of her way to get a closer look at her great-grandma.

At one point, she began asking my husband, Dennis, what happened to her great-grandmother's legs. Just as Assumma points out, that was the one aspect of this whole experience that just did not sit right with her.

"Most kids want to touch the person. They are not afraid. They are so at ease with it," Assumma says. "I have never had a problem with a child."

That said, he estimates that only 50 to 60 percent of families allow children to attend the wake and funeral services he directs—something he attributes to a culture that has tried to remove the reality of death from public view. It was not all that long ago that people died at home, and their wakes were often held in their homes. Children and adults were more at ease with and accepting of the idea of death because it was much more a part of normal life. Children saw grandparents, parents, even siblings, laid out in the living room as others kept vigil.

Those days are gone, and with them the healthy understanding that death is a sad but natural part of life.

Now we head to often-sterile funeral parlors where we can try to keep the image of death far from our homes and our daily lives. We attend services, send flowers, and offer prayers. But through it all we need to remember that wakes and funerals are much more than a polite way to honor the dead. They are a way to begin the grieving and the healing process—and that holds true for children as well as adults.

"There is a genuine need for us to see the physical remains. Our culture has gotten away from that," notes Assumma. "Death has been one of the greatest taboos. The reality is that we all go through it. It's a natural process in the cycle of life, and we don't teach our children that."

Funeral and memorial services allow children to acknowledge that it's OK to die. They help children understand that there is a process that people go through to grieve and to celebrate the life of the person who has died. To help that process along, chaplains, priests, ministers, funeral directors, pastoral ministers, counselors, teachers, and other caring adults can provide workbooks or other activities that will encourage children to express their feelings about death.

"Listen to your kids. Don't force them to go to the wake or funeral, but if they want to go and want to participate, let them. Almost all kids want to. Give them the opportunity," Assumma urges. "Our kids teach us brilliantly if we just watch them. Kids do know what's happening. It's foolish to think they don't. The kids know that something is wrong, and you cannot exclude them from it."

Preparing children for a wake or funeral

So, if we can't—or shouldn't—exclude children from the funeral home and the cemetery, how do we go about including them in the healthiest ways? The first step is to offer children the opportunity to attend the wake, funeral, or burial of a loved one or friend. Try to phrase the question in the most objective way possible so that you don't influence a decision one way or the other. Simply ask, "What do you think about going to the funeral with me?" If the answer is positive, the next step is to prepare the child for what she will see and hear.

The experience will vary greatly, depending on a child's age, the family's religious or ethnic customs, and the circumstances surrounding the death of the loved one. The best way to start a discussion on the subject is to begin with the basics: What is a funeral? What does the funeral home look like? What is a casket? What will be expected of the child once he or she is at the funeral home? What is cremation? What is a cemetery?

Toddlers, preschoolers, and other young children will want to know very simple details, such as what color the flowers will be, or whether there will there be any snacks or juice. They need to know how things will look when they enter the funeral home, why there are so many chairs lined up in rows, why people are writing in a special book, and why some people are laughing and others are crying.

It's best to stick to simple and truthful answers. Talk about the casket, and about why people send flowers. Ask if the child would like to send a flower arrangement in his name or if there is something else he would like to bring as a way of remembering Grandpa. Tell the child that he will have the chance to say a prayer near Grandpa, touch his hand, or simply sit in a chair nearby once he gets to the funeral home. Be sure to remind him that he doesn't have to do these things, but that he can do them if he wants.

The big questions that are likely to come from preschoolers and early elementary school children will have to do with the physical appearance of the deceased person. Explain to them that Grandma isn't breathing anymore, that her body doesn't work, that she can't hear or talk or feel anything. Her heart has stopped beating. She is dead. It may sound harsh, but direct answers that don't fuel active imaginations are the best way to begin the acceptance process.

Of course, explaining all this won't necessarily ensure that a child won't come up with some pretty outrageous ideas of his own—or that some well-meaning adult won't put some ideas in his head.

When my son was three years old, he attended the wake of an older woman we had known. I carefully went through all the proper explanations about her heart not beating and that even though she looked like she was sleeping, she was not. We answered every question he came up with at the funeral home and in the car. What I didn't know until later, however, was that the deceased woman's adult son kept telling Noah that she was "just sleeping." No sooner did we get in the car for the ride home when my son looked at me and asked, "Why was that lady sleeping in the big toy box?" My husband and I tried quickly and simply to explain one more time that she was not asleep, and then we let the matter drop.

It's not a bad idea to let friends and relatives know what you have told your child about death and about your deceased loved one. Otherwise you, too, may find your careful preparations undone in a matter of seconds by someone who has different ideas about what children should and shouldn't know.

Older children, because they have more knowledge, also have more fears. They may worry about what will happen once the body goes into the ground, or imagine that the person is not really dead and will be closed in the casket alive. Once again, it's best to be direct, truthful, and sensitive. Explain that Grandma was examined by a doctor and prepared by the funeral home staff before she was put in the casket. Let them know that there is no doubt about her being dead. Explain that the casket is designed to protect the body once it is in the ground, but that Grandma's soul has already moved on to the next life. Although her body will be there under the stone marker for years to come, her spirit is alive for all time. She is with God.

Questions from teens are probably the most difficult to field. Some may be designed to shock us, others to see if we are as steadfast in our religious beliefs as we claim to be. Remember that teenagers are in the already difficult position of trying to separate from parents and siblings. A death, especially the death of a close family member or friend, will create friction as they strive to maintain their independence and seek support at the same time. They may act indifferent. They may say they don't want to attend the funeral at all. Simply offer them the opportunity, and explain that they will not get another chance to say this particular kind of good-bye.

Involving children to make meaningful memories

If you are a member of the immediate family, you can arrange to go to the funeral home early so that your child can ask questions and view your loved one in private. If possible, talk to the funeral director ahead of time so that he is aware of your child's situation. Let him or her know if your child has ever been to a funeral before, if she has any understanding of what will happen at the funeral home, and if she has expressed either an interest in or a fear of participating.

Once your child has been told what to expect, take her by the hand and walk together to the casket. Kneel down beside it, if your child seems open to that suggestion, and talk about your loved one a bit before saying a prayer. Listen for cues from your child. She may have questions or worries that she wants to talk about, and it's OK to do that right there in front of the body.

Don't try to hold back your own emotions either. Your child will sense that something is wrong if you are desperately trying to keep from crying. Your child will learn from you that it is OK to cry and that feeling sad is normal. When your child sees that you are willing to let your feelings out, it opens the door for her to do the same.

Remember to ask your child if she wants to bring a photo or note or some other memento to leave behind in the casket. That in itself can be a healing act that will make the child feel forever connected in a physical way to the deceased loved one.

When my grandmother died two days before Christmas in 2014, Chiara was eight and had never been to a wake. She asked a lot of questions about why my grandmother's mouth looked the way it did, different from in life. She wondered aloud about whether her skin would feel like it did before. I told her she could touch my grandmother's hand or face, but she refrained. I touched my grandmother's forehead so that Chiara could see there was nothing scary about it. She knelt down and prayed, and, on the final morning before the funeral Mass, she brought along a picture she had made—a drawing of her standing side by side with my grandmother. Filled with hand-drawn hearts, the drawing included a simple message: "Rest in peace, E-ma." Chiara folded it up and slipped it in the casket with my grandmother. I smiled, remembering how I had done something similar when my other grandmother died thirty years before.

The funeral Mass or memorial service allows parents ample opportunities to involve children in concrete ways. Perhaps children can be altar servers or lectors. Maybe family members want to bring up the gifts during the offertory procession or sing a special song as part of the service.

I asked my son, Noah, if he wanted to read at my grandmother's funeral Mass. He is a lector at our home parish so I figured he'd be up for the task, and he seemed to be taking my grandmother's death fairly well. On top of that, he shares a New Year's Day birthday with her so they have a special connection. I assumed his refusal was due to some sort of teenage self-consciousness, but then he asked to be a pall bearer. I was confused; lector seemed so much more his style. Finally he confessed that he didn't think he could get through a reading without breaking down. His stoic teenage exterior was hiding the interior aching he didn't want anyone to see. And so he joined my husband and brother and other family members and carried my grandmother's casket in and out of the church, playing a role in the ritual on his own terms.

Father Terence Curley, who has written extensively about grief and loss, believes that the more everyone takes part in things, the better off they are. "The good thing about looking at life and death is that we're on a journey, and that metaphor of journey is very, very important. It's never too early to teach a child that there's a journey, and the journey is toward the kingdom of heaven."

Father Curley stresses that parents should not feel that they have to follow "a script." Rather, they should rely on their own instincts and deep and personal knowledge of their children. "I think we write the script as we go along. It's like any other subject. It's almost like you have to find out what a child's perception is and let him tell you. And if there's any resistance along the way, well, act appropriately," he explains. "Maybe he's not quite ready to go to a viewing or to a wake or a vigil, although by and large I recommend it."

"So the rule of thumb is that you have to know where your child is," Curley continues. "I think the parent is the best of all educators. The bond of love is greatest between the parent and the child. We have to rely on that. The parent has to rely on that as well. You just make your best judgment at the time, as long as the child feels safe and secure."

Graveside services, cremation, and the grieving process

Father Curley's advice also holds true for decisions about going to the crematory or attending the burial service. Some children may not be prepared for the idea of cremation or the visual memory of seeing a casket lowered into the ground. Others will be comforted by the fact that they have seen this process for themselves. They won't have to rely on more frightening images of cremation, cemeteries, and graves.

Peter Assumma suggests that the best way to talk to children about cremation is to focus on the natural process, not so much on the details of how it is performed. "Explain to them, in a sense, the story of *The Lion King*, the circle of life and how our body goes back to the earth. Cremation is just a much more rapid process than what we're used to," he says. "When I talk to folks, cremation is referred to as a 'radical' form of disposition—radical in the sense that the body is being brought to dust in a matter of hours as opposed to over a period of twenty years, as happens with a traditional burial."

Even fire, he explains, can have a positive connotation if we look at it as a source of heat and not an element of destruction. "Go toward that positive side, not speaking about fire but about how cremation is accelerating the process of returning the body to dust." In other words, cremation simply helps the natural process along.

That is also a good time to reiterate what we've already discussed—that a person who is dead cannot feel pain. When a loved one is cremated, we want to make sure our children understand that this process is not better or worse than traditional burial, just different. We can always turn to Scripture and remind them of the words from Genesis 3:19, which we hear every Ash Wednesday: "You are dust, and to dust you shall return."

Attending a burial, too, can be very traumatic for children. But experts say that the image often helps children move through the grieving process more quickly. In fact, many people find cemeteries to be comforting places to connect in a physical sense with the deceased loved one. Walk through any cemetery and you're likely to see everything from flowers and vigil lights to balloons and stuffed animals decorating the headstones. It's not uncommon to see people talking to their deceased loved ones at a cemetery. Then again, some people—and this holds true for children as well as adults—do not find comfort or peace or any connection at the cemetery. To them it is a sad reminder of what they have lost, not a place to talk.

Helping children see cemeteries as sacred, not scary

I have never found much meaning at the cemetery. It is the place where my mother's body is buried, but it is not the place where her spirit soars. I don't find a lot of comfort there. For my mother's sister, however, the cemetery is a place where she can be closer to my mother, where she can talk or remember happier times. It is a matter of personal taste, and as parents we should remember that our children may have the same strong feelings about cemeteries.

Ask your child what he thinks a cemetery is and what happens there. Let him ask questions, and answer them as simply and directly as possible. Ask him if he wants to go to the burial or the cemetery at a later date to leave flowers or some other token. Be open to whatever answer you get.

"We go to the cemetery a lot," says Carol Hyrcza, whose three-year-old son, Peter, drowned during a family outing in 1996. Her older son, Andrew, who was particularly close to Peter, often asks to go the cemetery to visit his brother's grave.

"When he has a bad day or doesn't feel that good about what's going on at school or something, he'll say, 'I need to go to the cemetery.' He'll just stand there. Sometimes he'll cry, and he'll say, 'I feel better now.' It's a pain that Andrew will always have and one I will always have. When Andrew cries, I try to tell him that we're just so lucky that we had Peter for as long as we did, that he had such a wonderful relationship with his brother."

If we are willing to include children in the rituals that are part of normal grief and mourning, we are likely to find that they are capable of handling so much more than we expect. Like Andrew Hyrcza, they may find comfort in the solitude of the cemetery. They may want to do all the things that we adults wish we could avoid. That's because children don't yet have all the fears and hang-ups we adults have about death.

When I took my son to my mother's grave back when he was only four years old, he climbed on the headstone with a complete lack of fear or concern. I was in awe of his matter-of-fact acceptance of our reality, his ability to grasp on some level that a woman he has never met, his grandmother, was buried there—and not be scared by it. All these years later, on the rare occasion that we are able to visit the cemetery during a visit to extended family, my children follow me from grave to grave, from my mother's grave to those of both sets of grandparents. Of these, they knew only my Italian grandmother.

They were there when she was buried on a cold December morning. They each placed a flower on her casket and said a prayer before turning to climb back into one of the cars in the long procession. From there, we made our way to a nearby restaurant, where we toasted my grandmother's life, hugged our relatives, and laughed about the many good times we shared with E-ma over the years. The juxtaposition of sorrow and joy, tears and laughter, grief and hope was both dramatic and comforting—a reminder that death can leave a gaping hole in our lives and leave us searching for meaning, but it never has the last word.

Preparing for a wake

Going to a funeral home for the first time can be a frightening experience for kids of all ages. They don't know what to expect. They imagine all kinds of things. We can help ease the fears by preparing them for what they will see.

Describe the physical atmosphere of the funeral home— what it looks like, if you expect a large crowd to be there, if there is a room designated for children who want to take a break from the viewing.

Explain what to expect once inside the viewing room. There will be many chairs for those paying respects. There will be a kneeler beside the casket for those who want to say a prayer and a final good-bye. Discuss whether the casket will be open or closed (if you know this information). Call ahead and ask the funeral director if he is willing to talk to your children privately before the viewing.

Let your child know that it's OK if he doesn't go up to the casket. On the other hand, also let him know that it's OK to lightly touch the person's hand or to leave a small memento in the casket as a farewell token.

Explain that most people will be talking quietly, but that others may be crying or laughing or talking loudly as they recall happy times they shared with the deceased loved one. Also explain that the immediate family (if you are not part of this group) will be greeting you in the viewing room. If you will be attending the wake on an evening when a clergy member will be leading prayers, explain this to your children so they are not confused or surprised.

Talk about why the wake is important. It is a way to say good-bye to a loved one, to celebrate her life, to honor her, and to mourn her. If children don't want to attend, don't push them. Allow them to come, or not come, to this gathering on their own terms.

Activity: Creating a Garden Memorial

Step 1. Help your child find a special spot—your loved one's favorite spot in the yard, a spot with a beautiful view, or a shady, peaceful spot just right for reflection.

Step 2. Clear a space for the memorial. The size of this space will depend on how elaborate you want the garden to be.

Step 3. Let your child choose a plant (or two or three) that was a favorite of your loved one or something that reminds you of that person—yellow roses because yellow was her favorite color, a lilac bush like the one outside her house, a small Norwegian spruce to remind you of her homeland. Selections also will depend on the climate and the sun or shade available in the location.

Step 4. Once the plants are in the ground, create a marker of some sort. It could be as simple as a rock you and your child discovered on a walk or as elaborate as a professionally made statue. It's up to you, but try to choose something in keeping with your loved one's personality.

Step 5. Make this spot a place where you and your child can come to reflect on your loved one's life, to cry when you are sad, and to laugh when you are happy. Water it, tend it, and enjoy it.

Additional ideas for your garden site:

Add a place for quiet contemplation— a large rock, a stone bench, or even a lawn chair. Your child may find that the spot becomes a favorite place to read, listen to music, or just observe nature.

Add other elements to expand and beautify the site. A bird feeder or birdbath might be nice, if your loved one was fond of birds, or a statue of St. Francis of Assisi or the Blessed Mother, wind chimes, a pinwheel, a wind sock, a small pond, or bubbling waterfall.

Create a personalized marker for the site— a stepping-stone with your child's handprints or pretty seashells or rocks embedded in it, a rock with your loved one's name or simply the word love or peace painted on it. Kits are available in craft stores, but it's not difficult to make your own with cement and plastic tubs or child-friendly paint and a rock from your yard.

If you don't have space outdoors, consider doing a smaller version as a container garden. Buy an inexpensive clay pot and let your child decorate it with paint or glitter. After the decorating is complete, add a couple of plants, some colored stones, seashells, a small statue, or some other small remembrance. Put it in a special spot in your home—maybe the place where you gather for prayer or on a table near a sunny window.

Questions for Reflection

» What is your first memory of visiting a funeral home? Were you scared? How do you think that first experience influenced your adult attitudes toward wakes and funerals?

» Reflect on the faith rituals we use to guide us through the initial days of grief and mourning. Are there ways to involve children in services, ceremonies, and liturgies that will give them some ownership in the process?

» Do you have any preconceived notions about children and wakes or funerals? Do you think children must be a certain age to attend, or conversely, do you believe an older child must attend?

» Can you take your child to the funeral of an elderly neighbor or distant relative to give her a first experience that will not be overly traumatic? Similarly, if you are not dealing with a recent death, can you take your child to a cemetery to visit the grave of a friend or relative so that her first experience is outside the parameters of fresh grief and traumatic loss?

Meditation: Saying Good-Bye

How do we say good-bye
to a piece of ourselves,
a life, a loved one, a friend,
whose absence leaves us
with an aching heart, an empty space?
We say it with the tears
that wash over us in waves,
with the prayers that serve as
a lifeline tossed into the sea of grief,
until little by little we reach a point
where we can say it with joy
for the blessing of the time we had,
with gratitude for the gift of love we shared.

10

Grief without Death: Special Circumstances

- Divorce, the loss that never ends
- Remarriage and revisiting sadness
- Military service and mixed emotions
- Relocating and readjusting

We live in a culture that mitigates genuine emotion of any kind, because it mitigates genuine anything. In a culture of denial, those who do not deny the depths of their feelings are often branded as fools or hysterics. . . . But grief suppressed will force its way to expression—whether we want it to or not.
—Marianne Williamson, *Everyday Grace*

Out on the periphery of typical grief and often unnoticed or unrecognized by parents and other adults is another kind of grief. This type grows out of losses that have nothing to do with death in a physical sense but everything to do with the death of a particular relationship or way of life. For children of divorce, there is the death of their family and the loss of the only life they've ever known. For children who are forced to move across the country, across the state, or even across their hometown, there is the loss of friends and relatives, a change of schools, a new house, a new neighborhood, a new normal. And for children whose parent is sent overseas for military service, there is not only the loss of a parent on the home front, but also the threat of constant danger and possible death and the uncertainty of never knowing when the separation will end.

Grief accompanies each of these types of loss. And although the grief is felt more sharply perhaps when the divorce is contentious or when a parent is serving in a dangerous military situation, all children who suffer similar family losses, even in the best of circumstances, do experience some level of grief. What makes this type of grief more difficult, in some ways, than the grief we recognize after a death is the lack of understanding about its reality. Many times people don't think of these situations as grief-inducing. As a result, children whose behavior changes due to this type of grief may not get an understanding response from parents and teachers and other adults. Also, because this type of grief doesn't involve a physical death, there are few support programs available to help children and parents learn to cope.

Divorce, the loss that never ends

"I see divorce very much as a grieving process," says Dianna Masto, a licensed clinical social worker who works with children. "In situations, particularly with a lot of conflict, I find it is very similar to dealing with a death, and in some ways it's actually worse. When there is ongoing fighting or when one kid has a conflict with one of the parents, it never ends."

Masto says that if the adults are working together and focusing on what's best for the children, then it can help minimize the grief, although it cannot prevent it entirely because divorce spells the death of a family. When parents are fighting constantly, however, or trying to turn children against the ex-spouse, divorce can lead not only to grief but also to developmental problems for children no matter what their age.

"It's like the loss that never ends. This constant fighting, this constant disruption. . . . Kids can't ever settle in and say this is the new normal because there's never any normal. Everything is always chaotic. It can rise to the level of trauma."

Masto says that even in the best divorce situation, children have to mourn their family. "Their family as they know it is gone, and they do have to make the adjustment to a new environment, whatever it is," she explains, adding that the role of parents is critical.

She has had some parents come to her in advance and ask how they should proceed with their divorce so that it has as little negative impact on their children as possible. On the flip side, some of her client families have gone back to court at least once a year, dragging children through repeated interviews with the law guardian. As a result, children are never able to move on because the crisis never ends.

Some children are even forced to pick sides during a divorce, something that creates "a tremendous block" between the child and the other parent. "It disrupts everything and disrupts them developmentally. You're not supposed to hate one parent and love the other parent. From a psychoanalytic standpoint, it's the absolute worst thing that can happen. It's a total disruption, and during adolescence, when you're already mad at your parents, this situation can allow you to focus all your anger on one of them. It disrupts the parents' ability to do a good job. It disrupts the developmental stuff. It really can be catastrophic," Masto explains.

Parents and other adults can be aware of the difficulties children of divorce may be facing, especially in the early days when there may be the initial separation from one parent, a move to a new location, the new reality of having two homes or, perhaps, seeing one parent only once or twice a week. As with grief from death, adults can watch for behavioral changes in these children—trouble eating or sleeping, nightmares or increased fears, changes in grades or interest in activities.

And, as with "typical" grief, the best antidote is dialogue. Talk to children, and listen to children. Tell them what they can expect to happen in the near future, and answer their questions. If children are kept in the dark about a family situation, they will begin to fill the void with their own storyline. Very often a child's imagination is worse than a parent's reality.

Remarriage and revisiting sadness

For children who have lost a parent to death or divorce, remarriage can trigger regrieving. Now the child is not just mourning the absence of a parent but grappling with the idea of a "replacement," at least on some level, for the missing parent.

In the case of remarriage after death, it can be especially difficult because a child may fear that his deceased parent is being forgotten. He may resent the stepparent because he thinks that if he likes this new parent it means he loves his dead parent less. This situation is fraught with challenges for children as they revisit the death of their parent and cope with the reality of having someone new—maybe someone they don't know that well yet—taking on the role of mother or father.

For children of divorce, remarriage will cause a different kind of regrieving. Perhaps they had continued secretly to hope that their parents would get back together, and the news of remarriage ends that hope and forces them to confront the separation anew. Even if parents had a contentious divorce and there was no hope for reconciliation, children often face an uphill battle trying to accept a new stepparent and learning to like and eventually love that person without feeling as if she is betraying the other parent, who may also be hurting from the news of an ex-spouse's remarriage.

For the parent who is remarrying, a child's resentment or anger can feel like intentional belligerence, which can set the stage for new problems between parent and child. Be aware that a child may be coping with a whole new stage of pain and confusion. Let him ask questions. Take time to listen. Do things together. For teachers and other adult caregivers, check in with children if you know they are adjusting to a change in their home life. If new or problematic behaviors surface, talk to parents so that everyone is on the same page.

Military service and mixed emotions

If divorce sets children up for a traumatic type of grief, military service trumps it. When a parent is sent overseas to serve in the military, children are forced to face not only the absence of a parent but the reality that every day is fraught with danger and there's no end in sight. On top of that, the parent at home is going through a similar grieving process and so might not be in the best position to give a child the attention she needs.

Although she says she's not an expert when it comes to the grief induced by military service, social worker Dianna Masto says this is the worst sort of grief without death, because of all the uncertainty.

"I have worked with one or two families dealing with this. The reality of having no idea what's going to happen and having the other adult at home dealing with these feelings as well makes it especially difficult. That's a whole other thing about grief: Kids can't necessarily depend on adults because they are grieving too," she says. "If I have to send someone significant in my life into battle, how am I going to parent my kids; how am I going to reassure them if it's a crisis for me?"

The ongoing uncertainty is what makes grief due to military deployment particularly difficult. "When somebody dies, you ultimately make peace with it and move on because there's certainty. You have to deal with it and figure out what to do to get through it. But in situations where there is no end, where there's constant uncertainty, you can't resolve the grief. There's no resolution," Masto says. "I hate to say that some grief is worse than others because obviously you can't measure or quantify it, but to me [grief over a parent 'lost' to military service] is the worst because there's no end. It just goes on and on. It's sort of like chronic illness."

According to the National Child Traumatic Stress Network, "military children experience unique challenges related to military life and culture," including parental separation due to deployment and reintegration of the family when deployment ends.

"Research also indicates that although most military children are healthy and resilient and may even have positive outcomes as a result of certain deployment stressors, some groups are more at risk," the Network states on its website. Among those it lists as at risk are young children, children with preexisting health issues, children whose families do not live close to military communities, children in single-parent families where the only parent has been deployed, and children in dual-military families where one or both parents have been deployed. The Network recommends that military parents seek out support from organizations that can help children deal with stress and "foster individual and family resilience."

Relocating and readjusting

When we moved our family years ago across the country from Austin, Texas, to Delmar, New York, one of our biggest concerns was for Noah, who had just turned four. He had recently begun attending a Montessori school he absolutely loved, and he had successfully adjusted to a new baby sister. Now we were asking him to adjust again—to a new town, a new climate, another new school, new friends, new everything.

At first he didn't seem to comprehend the finality of the move. He thought we were going back to Austin, that our house would be there waiting for us even though it had a new owner, that this journey was just an extended vacation. When reality set in, the problems began—not anything serious, but there were definite behavior changes. We could see it in the way Noah interacted with us, with his sister, Olivia, and with the kids in his new school. He got quieter. He wanted to be alone more often. He seemed angrier.

We did our best to help our son make this monumental adjustment. We painted his bedroom the exact same shade of blue as his bedroom in Austin. He hung up some of the same decorations. We enrolled him in the local Montessori school within weeks of our arrival. We talked often about our old home and his old school. We even created a journal about moving. This gave him a chance to list the best things about his old home and his new home and the worst things about both places. The exercise allowed him to see that everything about Austin wasn't wonderful and that everything about Delmar wasn't awful.

Six months after the move, his adjustment was complete. He loved his new school, his new room, and the snow that piled up around our doors and windows during the winter. He loved "our" museum and "our" farm. He would still talk about Austin, but usually it involved a possible vacation there to see his cousins. Because we let him run through the gamut of emotions—sadness, anger, disappointment, and, finally, joy—Noah could adjust to his new life on his own schedule. When he was upset, we acknowledged that this was a very difficult thing to go through. When he was sad, we honored it but reminded him that soon our new house would feel like home. We learned that we couldn't force anything. We had to take our cues from Noah.

Often his comments surprised us, like the time we were cooking pancakes and he said, "This is the first time we're having pancakes—in this house." I knew he was thinking about his old life in Austin. This remark allowed me to reminisce with him and also talk about how exciting it was to be doing this for the first time in our new home. It was through our ordinary activities that Noah expressed his extraordinary worries and fears. Children are not going to make appointments to sit down and talk frankly about their concerns. They are going to see something that sparks a question, eat something that brings back a memory, go somewhere that causes them to break into tears—or into laughter. If we make a point to be there *with* them, we can be there *for* them.

"Moving can be difficult, especially for young children in preschool or early elementary school. They don't like disruption, and they don't feel fully safe outside of home," explains Dianna Masto. "I don't know if it rises to the level of grief, but it definitely requires an adjustment." She notes that children may begin to have nightmares and sleep disruptions, and sadness may surface at different times on any given day.

On its website, healthychildren.org, the American Academy of Pediatrics (AAP) suggests that parents focus on positive aspects of their move, such as the excitement of learning about a new city and meeting new friends. "Children tend to think about the negative side when a family moves. There is the loss of friends and, along with it, loss of a sense of belonging. In the new community the children will be newcomers, strangers, and may need to learn some different social rules," the AAP states, adding that children need time and space to adjust to their new reality:

> Give your child adequate notice to get used to the idea of moving—even a year in advance may be appropriate. Acknowledge her sadness about leaving behind friends and familiar places. Let her know you are sympathetic and that you understand that she might feel nervous about what awaits her, whether it is the new people, the new school, or the new bus ride.

Activity: Keeping Connections

Use the following journaling suggestions to help children who are facing a loss due to separation rather than death. By recording the events of his days—to be shared with a loved one or friend at a later date—a child can maintain that important sense of connection.

1. Let your child pick out a journal. It could be a simple spiral notebook or a pretty hardcover book with special paper. If your child is older or technologically savvy, the journal could be digital. If you go the digital route, the sky's the limit in terms of recording moments in words, images, and video.

2. If your child is younger, give her suggestions for things to include: highlights from school, special moments from favorite activities or sports, daily moments that remind her of her absent parent. She can glue in photos, ticket stubs, report cards, and other memorabilia.

3. If you are the absent parent, keep a journal for your child. Fill it with interesting details from your days apart. This is especially good for a child whose parent is deployed. When the two are finally reunited, parent and child can exchange journals and catch up on what was missed. In the case of relocation, suggest that a relative or friend left behind in your old community keep a journal for your child to be shared on your next visit.

Questions for Reflection

» Have you sat down with your child and talked about her changing home life? What positive things can you emphasize? What fears can you address?

» Is your child exhibiting any new or problematic behaviors since the loss of his former life, whether due to divorce, remarriage, military deployment, or relocation? Anything dangerous—drug abuse, self-harm, talk of suicide—requires an immediate phone call to your doctor, a counselor, and a support program.

» If you are in a divorce situation, can you and your ex-spouse talk about ways to minimize the negative impact on your children?

» If a parent is being deployed, can you have an honest conversation with your children about what's going to happen? If you don't know your return date, don't give them false hopes by telling them a time frame that may be unrealistic. Can you give your child enough information without fanning their fears?

» If you are relocating your family, can you involve the children in finding a new home? If they can't visit your new community in person, can you let them take a virtual tour online?

Meditation: Outside the Lines

All the pieces are still here
and yet something is missing.
I keep moving forward, keep looking ahead,
but I long for the life I knew,
a life that made me feel whole.
Things are not the same anymore,
but that doesn't mean
I can't find joy right where I am.
I can still create a rainbow,
even if I have to color outside the lines.

Appendix A: Support for Teachers, Counselors, and Other Adult Helpers

If you're an adult on the frontlines of a child's life outside the home—teacher, counselor, coach, babysitter, day care worker—it's very likely that you will be thrown into a difficult grief situation at some point, perhaps without even knowing that a death has occurred. You may suddenly notice that a child has become weepy or fearful or is no longer able to pay attention. If a parent hasn't told you the specifics of what's going on, it can be hard to know what's at the heart of the new behavior. In situations where a national tragedy or natural disaster or some other especially horrific and public death occurs, you may be blindsided by a barrage of questions from your students and unsure of how to assuage their fears and answer their questions. Grief can be an emotional land mine, and for adult helpers trying to navigate it with only some of the information, it can be nearly impossible for everyone to get out unscathed.

To thine own self be true

David Aaker, author (with Jan Nelson) of *The Bereavement Ministry Program* and pastor of St. Paul Lutheran Church in Le Center, Minnesota, has been involved in bereavement ministry for more than forty years. When it comes to helping others deal with grief, he often refers to a quote by Quaker author Parker Palmer: "Violence arises when we don't know what to do with our suffering."

"If you and I don't listen to the grief or the suffering that a person who has experienced the death of a loved one is feeling, if we don't listen, that turns into violence. It turns into becoming totally disengaged, or it turns into drinking or drugs or any number of things that any of us can get involved in if we don't find ways of dealing with that suffering," he explains. And that goes for children as well as adults.

So how can adults listen to the grief and suffering of children in their care? It begins with an inward look.

"You can listen to another person's story only to the extent that you listen to your own story," Aaker says, recalling the words of one of his long-ago mentors. "I remember from personal experience, when I moved to New York City, it had been shortly after my own father's death. I was not able to listen to my own story. If you started to talk about your father's death, I would change the subject and talk about my father's death. I can listen to your pain only to the extent that I have listened to my own pain."

So now is the time to focus on your own story, to face your own pain. If you can do it before you have to help a child through grief, you'll be better able to hear what they're saying and know what they need without tangling up their feelings with your own feelings. Aaker stresses the importance of self-care, especially for those who are involved in grief counseling or bereavement ministry on a regular basis, which can begin to take an emotional toll. Take time for yourself. Go for a walk, meditate, read a novel, take a lunch break and meet a friend, anything that will refill your own depleted store of energy and peace.

Try to see through their eyes

Sometimes we adults can forget how things look or sound to a child. A girl who's lost her mother goes to a Girl Scout meeting where everyone is decorating Mother's Day cards and begins to act out or break down. Her mom may have died a year ago, or even a few years ago, but that event could trigger something that sets her back. If we can put ourselves in that child's shoes and try to imagine what that must feel like, we're no longer surprised by the aggressive behavior or withdrawn demeanor or total disinterest.

Remember that every child will grieve differently. Where one child might do all the things you might expect of someone in grief expressed through outward sadness or crying, another child might want to run around outside or play music or spend time with friends. It doesn't mean that child isn't grieving, only that he expresses his grief and alleviates his pain in different ways. So we can't be judgmental when dealing with children coping with death and loss. Every kind of grief is the right kind of grief, even when it's unconventional or unexpected or unfamiliar to us.

Here's what the Dougy Center recommends:

One of the most helpful and healing things we can do for a child is to listen to his or her experiences without jumping in to judge, evaluate, or fix. Well-meaning adults often try to comfort a child with phrases such as, "I know just how you feel," or worse, advice such as "get over it" or "move on." While our intentions to soothe a grieving child are correct, such responses negate the child's own experiences and feelings. If a child says, "I miss my Dad who died," simply reflect back what you've heard, using their words, so they know that they're being listened to. Use open-ended questions such as "What's that been like?" or "How is that?"; children are more likely to share their feelings without pressure to respond in a certain way.

See parents as partners

If you are a teacher or regular care provider, your best insights into the worries of a child in your care will come from her parents. By keeping lines of communication open, you'll know if and when a child may be struggling with something particularly difficult. If you notice behaviors that are troublesome or out of the ordinary, contact parents to ask if there's anything unusual going on at home. Often parents don't realize that something as "minor" as the death of a pet can have a huge impact on a child.

When you first meet parents, let them know that it's always best if they can inform you of any changes at home before a child returns to school or day care. Remind them that parental separation (even for a short time), moving, and certainly deaths of any kind whether close to home or far removed are likely to affect a child even if he isn't saying anything obvious. Ask parents to keep you in the loop, even if it's just to send you a quick e-mail update when a change or loss has occurred.

In the case of a public tragedy that has been in the news, let parents know if you'll be discussing things in class. Tell them what you plan to say ahead of time so they, in turn, have time to address the issue at home first.

When to seek or suggest outside assistance

Unless you are a trained grief counselor, there may come a time when a child's grief is simply more than you can—or should—handle. Even those who are trained counselors sometimes have to call in doctors and other medical professionals, such as when children are making suicidal comments, showing signs of self-harm, or getting involved in activities that are dangerous, such as drug use or sexual promiscuity. When these more extreme grief reactions surface, seek professional support and outside assistance immediately.

Appendix B: Exercises and Activities for Parents and Children

Create a Collage

This a simple but powerful exercise that will allow a child to be creative while having the chance to reflect on their loved one.

- You'll need some sturdy paper or poster board (8½ x 11 is fine), three or four old magazines, scissors, and a glue stick.

- Give your child a clean, flat work space in a quiet room. Tell her to start paging through magazines and cutting out any words or images that make her think of her deceased loved one. It can be a large picture or a small, single word taken out of a larger passage or ad. Anything is fair game.

- Once she has finished going through the magazines, tell her to start gluing pieces down. She can methodically plan the collage out, choosing just the right spot or angle, or she can glue randomly.

- Sit down with your child and talk about the collage. Ask what certain things mean, why she chose particular words or images, whether there was a reason certain things were grouped together.

- If she'd like, have her write down what she was thinking and feeling as she made the collage. Date it so that someday down the road she can look back and remember what she was feeling at the time.

- If your child would like to display the collage, pick up some Mod Podge at a craft store, and paint on a thin layer. This will keep items from peeling up. You can even frame it and let your child hang it in her room or some other prominent place in your home.

Memory Makers

Recording memories in some fashion is a great exercise. Let a child use his imagination, or take ideas from the list below and adapt them to an individual child or situation.

Create a Memory Mobile. Select seashells, pinecones, pictures, trinkets, or any small mementos of a loved one that have special meaning. Tie the items to pieces of yarn cut at various lengths. Tie the other ends of the yarn to the bottom of a clothes hanger. A child can suspend the mobile from his bedroom ceiling, providing a visible reminder of your loved one.

Create a Memory Box. This is an especially nice idea if your child has actual items from a loved one that are too big or too bulky to paste into a book. Take a shoe box or buy a small plastic box and allow your child to decorate the outside with paints, stickers, fabric, wallpaper, contact paper, and/or photos. Line the inside with tissue paper, wrapping paper, or fabric. Allow your child to include small items that remind her of your loved one—a special rock, a lapel pin, photos, a prayer book, a pressed flower. Your child can take the box out and look at the items whenever she is missing your loved one.

Create a Bookmark. This is an especially simple activity—good for very young children or those who are not as interested in artistic endeavors. Find a favorite photo of your loved one. Have your child glue the photo to a piece of colored paper or cardboard. Let him write your loved one's name, birth year, and death year under the photo (or write it for him). An older child may want to write a poem or include a quote from your loved one's favorite poem. Use clear contact paper to cover the bookmark. Your child can use the bookmark in a favorite book, journal, or prayer book.

Creating a memorial for a pet

Over the years our family has had to bury two dogs, Chester and Greta, and a cat, Hamlet. We've seen how children—and parents—of all different ages and stages struggle with the loss of a beloved animal. There were tears of sadness over the good friend lost and tears of joy over happy times recalled. There were touching good-byes in our backyard and loving remembrances around our house. All of it helped us and our children get past the loss without losing the memories.

- Create the memorial in your yard.
- Mark the spot with flowers or a statue.
- Write your pet's name on a stone or a piece of wood and use it as a marker. We have two small white rectangular stones sticking up out of the ground in a patch of irises and hostas at the edge of our backyard to mark the graves of Greta and Hamlet. In addition, we have a St. Francis of Assisi statue that stands above the flowers and plants so that even in the middle of summer, we don't lose sight of the memorial garden. We can even see it from our deck and from our kitchen windows, so we are constantly reminded of our furry friends.
- Gather the family around the memorial site and have each family member share a story about your pet. We did this with all of our pets, but the time that stands out most was the day we buried our cat, Hamlet. I remember the kids putting yarn and some treats

into the box with him before my husband lowered it into the ground (out of the sight of our children since that might have been a little too traumatic). Once Hamlet was covered with dirt, we gathered around the grave and said a prayer.

- Place flowers on the site on the anniversary of your pet's death, on the day she was born, or on the day you brought her home.

Alternate pet memorials.

- Ask your vet if there is any way to get a plaster mold of your pet's paw. Our vet in Texas gave us a small plaster cast of Chester's paw, and it still sits on the shelf in our living room. Every time we dust or pull out a book, we think of Chester. If you can't get a mold, frame a favorite photo and put it somewhere prominent.
- Create a keepsake that is small enough to fit in your child's pocket or under her pillow—a piece of your dog's favorite blanket, your cat's identification tag, a small stone with your pet's name written on it, anything that your child can hold onto whenever she's missing her pet.
- Have your child write down some thoughts about her pet either in a journal or in letter form.
- Create a Christmas ornament by having your pet's name, birth year, and death year etched on an ID tag at the pet store. Loop a piece of yarn through it and hang it on your tree each year.

A digital diary

If your child prefers technology and digital communication over handwritten journals and arts and crafts projects, allow him to create a digital diary or scrapbook.

Find an application that will work for whatever technology your child can access—personal computer, laptop, tablet, or smartphone.

The options are constantly changing and advancing every day, so look around for what works best for your child.

If you have a lot of photos of your loved one, create a slide show and watch it as a family. You can also import the photos into a calendar or book layout and have it printed as a keepsake.

Create a video "scrapbook." Ask family members to talk "on camera" about their favorite memories of your loved one. Visit your loved one's favorite places and shoot video as you narrate what you're seeing. Pick some meaningful music to play in the background. Teenagers are especially adept at using technology to create these kinds of projects. Even if you think it sounds too difficult, chances are your teen will take to it intuitively.

Appendix C: Resources for Healing

Recommended Reading for Parents and Other Adult Helpers Who Are Guiding a Child through Grief

A Grief Unveiled: One Father's Journey through the Death of a Child, by Gregory Floyd, Paraclete Press, 1999. A father's moving story of his journey through grief after the death of his six-year-old son.

How to Go On Living When Someone You Love Dies, by Therese A. Rando, Bantam Books, 1991. Another classic that talks about death and grief in general, with a specific section on children and grief.

Six Steps for Managing Loss: A Catholic Guide through Grief, by Terence P. Curley, Alba House, 1997. A guidebook based on faith. Includes exercises for managing loss and a section on personal prayer.

Talking about Death: A Dialogue between Parent and Child, by Earl Grollman, Beacon Press, 1990. A classic that gives specific examples of how to talk to a child about death.

Wish You Were Here: Travels through Loss and Hope, by Amy Welborn, Image, 2012. Especially good for those who have lost a spouse and are helping young children face their grief.

Recommended Reading for Children Ages Four to Eight

The Fall of Freddie the Leaf, by Leo F. Buscaglia, Holt Rinehart Winston, 1982. The story of a leaf serves as a parable that sheds light on the mysteries of life and death.

I'll Always Love You, by Hans Wilhelm, Crown, 1985. A wonderful book that focuses on life and love through the story of a dog's death.

Lifetimes: The Beautiful Way to Explain Death to Children, by Bryan Mellonie and Robert Ingpen (Contributor), Bantam Books, 1983. This book uses the cycles of nature to talk about death. A good primer for those who want to bring up the subject ahead of time.

Sad Isn't Bad: A Good-Grief Guidebook for Kids Dealing with Loss, by Michaelene Mundy, R.W. Alley (Illustrator), Abbey Press, 1998. A wonderful book by a mother, teacher, and school counselor. Helps children explore the many scary feelings and questions that death and grief bring up.

Saying Goodbye to Daddy, by Judith Vigna, Albert Whitman & Co., 1991. A good book about a sad subject—a dad who dies in a car accident.

Talking about Death, by Karen Bryant-Mole, Raintree Steck-Vaughn, 1999. A good primer for kids who are learning about death or dealing with their own reactions after the loss of a loved one.

What's Heaven? by Maria Shriver, Sandra Speidel (Illustrator), Golden Books, 1999. A mother and daughter talk about heaven following the death of a beloved great-grandmother.

When Dinosaurs Die: A Guide to Understanding Death, by Laurie Krasny Brown and Marc Tolon Brown (Illustrator), Little Brown & Company, 1996. Addresses children's fears about death.

When a Pet Dies, by Fred Rogers, Putnam, 1988. A basic and helpful book by one of public television's most beloved figures.

Recommended Reading for Children Ages Nine to Twelve

I Will Remember You: My Catholic Guide through Grief, by Kimberly B. Schuler, Mary Joseph Peterson (Illustrator), Pauline Books and Media, 2011. An activity book for children ages seven through twelve.

Sky Memories, by Pat Brisson, Wendell Minor (Illustrator), Delacorte Press, 1999. A beautiful book about the death of a single mother written from her daughter's perspective.

What on Earth Do You Do When Someone Dies? by Trevor Romain, Free Spirit Press, 1999. Suggests ways of dealing with questions of loss that frequently come up.

When Someone Dies, by Sharon Greenlee, Bill Drath (Illustrator), Peachtree Publishers, 1992. A teacher and grief counselor explores a tough subject.

Recommended Reading for Teens and Young Adults

The Grieving Teen: A Guide for Teenagers and Their Friends, by Helen Fitzgerald, Simon & Schuster, 2000. Renowned grief counselor focuses on the special needs of adolescents in grief.

Straight Talk about Death for Teenagers: How to Cope with Losing Someone You Love, by Earl A. Grollman, Beacon Press, 1993. Rabbi and grief expert uses prose-poem format to help teens coping with death of a family member or friend.

Recommended Reading for Parish Leaders, Funeral Directors, and Others Who Deal with Bereaved Children

The Bereavement Ministry Program: A Comprehensive Guide for Churches, by Jan Nelson and David Aaker, Ave Maria Press, 1998, 2009. Good for anyone involved in regular grief counseling or bereavement ministry, especially on a parish level.

Console One Another: A Guide for Christian Funerals, by Terence P. Curley, Sheed & Ward, 1993. Describes how a parish community can minister to bereaved members. Includes scriptural suggestions, prayers for special circumstances, and a section on how to discuss death with children.

The Ministry of Consolation: A Parish Guide for Comforting the Bereaved, by Terence P. Curley, Alba House, 1993. Chapter 3 focuses on "Grief through the Eyes of a Child."

Recommended Reading for Specialty Areas

After Miscarriage: A Catholic Woman's Companion to Healing & Hope, by Karen Edmisten, Servant Books, 2012.

A Piece of My Heart: Living through the Grief of Miscarriage, Stillbirth, or Infant Death, by Molly Fumia, Conari Press, 2000.

Bart Speaks Out: Breaking the Silence on Suicide, by Linda Goldman, Western Psychological Services, 1998.

Breaking the Silence: A Guide to Helping Children with Complicated Grief—Suicide, Homicide, AIDS, Violence, and Abuse, 2nd ed., by Linda Goldman, Brunner-Routledge, 2002.

Figuring Sh!t Out: Love, Laughter, Suicide, and Survival, by Amy Biancolli, Behler Publications, 2014. A powerful book that tackles the subject of suicide with wit, wisdom, and incredible honesty.

Grief Support Organizations

The Compassionate Friends
P.O. Box 3696
Oak Brook, IL 60522-3696
Phone: 877-969-0010 (toll free)
Fax: 630-990-0246
www.compassionatefriends.org

The Dougy Center
The National Center for Grieving Children and Families
P.O. Box 86852
Portland, OR 97286
Phone: 503-775-5683
www.dougy.org

The Christi Center
2306 Hancock Drive
Austin, TX 78756
Phone: 512-467-2600
www.christicenter.org

Ferncliff Camp and Conference Center
1720 Ferncliff Road
Little Rock, AR 72223
Phone: 501-821-3063
E-mail: ferncliff@gmail.com
www.ferncliff.org

Fernside
Supporting Children and Families through Grief
4360 Cooper Road, Suite 100
Cincinnati, OH 45242
Phone: 513-246-9140
www.fernside.org

National Alliance for Grieving Children
900 SE Ocean Blvd.
Suite 130D
Stuart, FL 34994
Telephone: 866-432-1542
www.childrengrieve.org

The Warm Place
Grief Support Center for Children
809 Lipscomb Street
Fort Worth, TX 76104-2710
Phone: 817-870-2272
E-mail: info@thewarmplace.org
www.thewarmplace.org

Other Websites to Visit for Advice

www.aacap.org American Academy of Child & Adolescent Psychiatry.
Search "child and grief" for information and recommendations.

www.beliefnet.org Beliefnet has articles, columns, and discussions on
all aspects of grief. Search for "grief and loss."

www.centerforloss.com Site of the Center for Loss and Life Transition,
run by renowned grief expert Dr. Alan Wolfelt.

www.drgreene.com Pediatrician Alan Greene answers parents' questions about grief and other parenting issues.

www.focusonthefamily.com Focus on the Family website with specialized grief page. Search "How to Help Your Child Grieve."

www.kidsaid.com Part of GriefNet, an Internet community for people dealing with grief and loss, this site offers a "frequently asked questions" section for children and adults, as well as poetry, stories, and a "kid-to-kid" support network.

www.healthychildren.org American Academy of Pediatrics with specialized information for children adjusting to relocation.

www.nctsn.org The National Child Traumatic Stress Network with specialized information for military families.

Acknowledgments

I have to begin these acknowledgments with my editor at Loyola Press, Joe Durepos. He saw something timeless and valuable in the original version of this book and encouraged me to revise and update it for a brand new audience. It is such a gift to know that my first book will see a new life. Even after all these years, this project has remained close to my heart because it contains so many personal stories and memories. As I reviewed and rewrote, I was taken back to sorrowful but significant times, and, because of that, people long gone from my life suddenly felt much closer.

I also need to thank my current editor, Vinita Wright, and my original editor at Loyola Press, Jim Manney, who enthusiastically supported this book through proposals, outlines, writing, and editing the first time around, as well as independent editor Evelyn Bence, whose insights helped me immensely.

On the home front, I am blessed to be able to say that the people I thanked when I wrote the original version of this book in 2002 are the very same people I need to thank today. My husband, Dennis, is always an integral part of any book project I undertake. He cheers me on, offers professional advice, and cooks dinner when I'm in my basement office well past closing time trying to nail down one last

interview or wrap up one last chapter. I couldn't ask for a better partner and best friend.

I have to admit that I've always felt bad that the original version
of this book didn't include our youngest child in the dedication. She
didn't come along until three years after publication, but somehow it
just seemed wrong. Now I get to rectify that. So a big thank you to our
children, Noah James, Olivia Irene, and Chiara Elizabeth for always
being excited about my writing.

About the Author

Mary DeTurris Poust is a writer, retreat leader, and author of six books, including *Everyday Divine: A Catholic Guide to Active Spirituality* and *Cravings: A Catholic Wrestles with Food, Self-Image, and God*. She writes about the spiritual journey on her blog, Not Strictly Spiritual, and in her monthly column, Life Lines. She lives with her husband, Dennis, and their three children in upstate New York. Visit her website at www.NotStrictlySpiritual.com.

Also Available

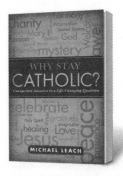

Why Stay Catholic?
Unexpected Answers to a
Life-Changing Question

MICHAEL LEACH
$14.95 • Paperback • 3537-5

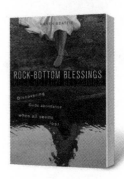

Rock-Bottom Blessings
Discovering God's Abundance
When All Seems Lost

KAREN BEATTIE
$13.95 • Paperback • 3842-0

The Thorny Grace of It
And Other Essays for
Imperfect Catholics

BRIAN DOYLE
$14.95 • Paperback • 3906-9

Continue the Conversation

If you enjoyed this book, then connect with Loyola Press to continue the conversation, engage with other readers, and find out about new and upcoming books from your favorite spiritual writers.

Visit us at **LoyolaPress.com** to create an account and register for our newsletters.

Or scan the code on the left with your smartphone.

Connect with us through:

 Facebook
facebook.com
/loyolapress

 Twitter
twitter.com
/loyolapress

 **YouTube**
youtube.com
/loyolapress